T0196554

Railway Babu:
My Father

Satya P. Sharma

*author*HOUSE®

AuthorHouse™
1663 Liberty Drive
Bloomington, IN 47403
www.authorhouse.com
Phone: 1 (800) 839-8640

Published by AuthorHouse 03/28/2016

ISBN: 978-1-5246-0080-8 (sc)
ISBN: 978-1-5246-0079-2 (e)

Library of Congress Control Number: 2016905132

Portrait of Baoji by the Author

Dedicated to my late father, Shri Kundan Lal Sharma
(born November 26, 1904, died February 14, 1963),

and my late mother, Mohar Devi Sharma
(born January 4, 1907, died June 28, 1992)

You gave me life. This is the least I could do.

ACKNOWLEDGEMENTS

My retirement in 2014 provided me the opportunity to write this novel, my first, that I always wanted to write. Soon after I retired, I bought a condo in Surrey, British Columbia and spent five months there during the winter of 2014-15. In my solitude there I conceived of this novel, created a format and an outline for it, and started writing. Moving back to Saskatoon to sell my house, I continued the effort there. I also did the writing during my trip to New Zealand and Australia during May-June of 2015. I also wrote a number of pages aboard planes and airports. But the bulk of the writing was done in Saskatoon.

I take full responsibility for my shortcomings as a writer. But for factual accuracy and confirmation of some details I frequently consulted my brother, Jagat Sharma. He showed great interest in this project and I thank him for his invaluable help.

PROLOGUE

There are few novels where the author describes the life of his/her father. At least I have not read any. In my retirement now, I often think of my parents. How against such heavy odds, they were able to raise a large family, doing the very best they could with very limited resources. This is probably the story of many lower middle class families of India that came into existence in the early decades of the twentieth century.

My father had a complex personality that was more than likely shaped by the various struggles in his life. He was the first child of his parents. I never saw his mother, my *Dadi*. She died rather young, only in her thirties. She gave birth to several children, but only four survived: my father, my uncle, Ram Kumar, my *Bhua* (aunt), Kaushalya, who lived for many years after her two brothers had passed away, and another uncle, Rishi, but he died at the age of 16. My mother was only 15 when she married my father. She became a mother at age 17. Soon after her marriage, *Dadi* passed away, leaving very young Rishi behind. My mother breast-fed both her first son and Rishi, her brother-in-law. This was not totally uncommon those days. She was very close to Rishi who she raised like her own son. She often talked about Rishi even twenty years after he had passed away.

My father, Baoji as we called him, was a man of many moods. He was also a very religious and emotional human being. He could be the happiest man at a given moment. When angry, he could shout at the top of his voice. When upset or sad, he could cry loudly. He could not hide his emotions. He loved all his children and felt it his duty to raise them the best way he could. He knew the importance of education and wanted all his children to excel in education. He expected all his children to succeed in studies and set very high standards for them: If you do not get first division you are as good as a failure. That motivated all his children. Only Hari could not do as well as the others in his younger years.

Although an orthodox Brahman, Baoji defied many Brahman norms. He drank, smoked, and ate meat, the latter being totally forbidden in the house by my mother. Baoji went through many ups and downs in his life. Because of his inability to support all his children financially, he surrendered his patriarchal authority to his oldest son, the latter becoming the anchor for all the siblings in the city of Delhi, with the exception of my elder sister, Binno, who was married very young at the age of 15. Binno was also deprived of any formal education.

Baoji, throughout his later life, believed that his oldest son had usurped his patriarchal authority. Often he resented it. This resentment often came out in loud outbursts when he was drunk. Sometimes, he talked to himself. On occasions, he found comfort in hugging his cow that he loved as his mother.

Eventually, my father came down with cancer that was diagnosed rather late. He died at age of 58 in Delhi, on February 14, 1963. That was the saddest day of my life. I thought my life had ended. How could a robust, tall, handsome man weighing over 200 pounds, be reduced to a mere skeleton and die so young? When all the siblings flourished and made successful careers in their chosen fields, Baoji was no longer there. How many times I wish he had seen our prosperity. The Valentine Day, his day of passing, always brings sadness to me. I will miss Baoji as long as I live.

This is my first novel. I hope the readers will appreciate the love, pathos, and compassion that Baoji imparted. It will also serve as a family chronicle for my children and grandchildren as well as members of my extended family.

Contents

1

BULLANDSHEHAR

A lovable man my father was. Like everyone else in the large family he created, he was a man of many contradictions. An orthodox Hindu who kept a *choti,* a long flock of hair at the back of his head, larger than the rest of his head, who wore a *janeo* (sacred thread) on his body like many orthodox high caste Hindus and worshipped everyday after a bath, sitting cross-legged with folded hands on a *chauki* (a medium height table), eyes closed and the mouth frequently uttering some words in soft tone barely audible, he looked like a saint in early mornings. Out of his six children, my younger sister and I spent most time with him in my early years. Yet, every night he will drink country liquor, often diluted with water by my mother. Tuesdays were an exception. He was a devotee of Hanuman, the monkey-shaped Hindu god and kept a fast that day. Drinking liquor was off limit that day.

All the children called him *Baoji.* A usually quiet man during daytime, he became animated and came alive soon after he had a drink or two. He was a railroad employee in Northern Indian Railway, first as assistant station master, and later in his career as stationmaster, he moved almost every two to three years, getting transferred from one railway station to another. Being a 'railway child' I loved trains. Trains of all types: freight trains, passenger trains, express trains, and mail trains. Many of my childhood hobbies were related to trains, railway platforms, train signals, and watching trains come and go. From Baoji I learned a lot about his job. He taught me how to send telegraphs….grr-gut…grr-gut,…gut-grr; how to unload the round metal ball tokens from the slot machines; he even would allow me to sell train tickets under his supervision. We were after all a railway family. My grandfather (on my father's side) was a stationmaster, his younger brother was in railways also, as was my uncle (my father's younger brother), being a goods clerk. I was told that my great grandfather was a police inspector, an odd job for a Brahman.

Baoji only studied enough to matriculate. At first, he worked with the meter gaze, BB&CI Railways, that is Bombay, Baroda, and Central Indian Railways, as an assistant stationmaster. He was already married then to Amma, my mother, who came from a rich, landowning family from a village on the border of Rajasthan and Punjab (now Haryana when the State of Haryana was created out of Punjab in 1968 on basically linguistic grounds, Punjab for Punjabi speakers, and Haryana for Hindi speakers). A few years into the job, there was a mishap: a train accident occurred during Baoji's duty hours. Assistant stationmasters worked eight-hour night shifts, from 4 pm to 12 midnight or from midnight to 8 am. Only the stationmaster worked during the 8 am to 4 pm day shift. My father was drunk on duty, entertaining a relative at home. He asked the porter to give the signal for a coming train. The porter made a mistake in giving the wrong signal and the oncoming train collided with the stationary train parked near the platform.

Baoji was fired from his job. He struggled for a few years in our native town, working as a letter writer near the court.

When the Northern Indian Railway, with broad gaze, opened, Baoji found a job again as assistant station master at a small railway station, Dadri, in western Uttar Pradesh. He worked in Uttar Pradesh for the rest of his life. Many train stations: Dadri, Allahabad, Garhmukteshwar, Khurja City, Bullandshehar, Hapur, Gajraula, Umartali, Hapur again, Simbhaoli, Balawali, and Makhi. My oldest brother was born in Bawal, our hometown. The next two brothers were born in Dadri, my older sister in Allahabad, myself in Khurja City, and my younger sister (the last child) in Bullandshehar.

My Amma gave birth to many kids. She actually conceived 10 times. Her first four children were all boys but they all died young. Infant mortality was very high in India in the early decades of the twentieth century. Amma was a tough, hardy woman, with a temper, but highly compassionate. She was the manager of the family and ran the household in her style. How she made ends meet on Baoji's meager salary was something she only knew. All her kids learned fiscal management from her. In 1950 Baoji's monthly salary was a meager 115 rupees. To bring up six children and educate them was well nigh impossible. So Baoji and Amma made some tough decisions. The oldest brother, Amar, was sent for his B.A. at Meerut College where he also stayed in a hostel. The next two brothers, Hari and Rajiv, were sent to Rewari, a bigger town where our Chachaji (uncle) lived working as a goods clerk in the railway. Ram Kumar Chachaji had no kids of his own and he and Chachiji (his wife) were happy to take care of Hari and Rajiv who did their High School in Rewari.

My older sister, Binno, the younger sister, Karuna, and I lived with Baoji and Amma in Gajraula. Baoji had some *ooper ki amdani* (extra income) that he got by selling passes to milkmen traveling by train, the vendors who sold their sweets, snacks, tea, *paan* (betel leaf), etc. One could legitimately call it bribe but this was the norm in most walks of life back then, and still is in modern day India. In Gajraula, he had credit accounts with the sweet shop and the milkman, and paid them at his convenience. Despite occasional misunderstandings, Amar was Baoji's favourite and he had high expectations of him. But Amar had developed some bad habits through the company he kept. Although he had artistic talent, he got addicted to gambling during his college days in Meerut. He used to play the card game of *teen patti* (three card Indian poker). He could play this game with anyone who was ready to bet money on it, even the *Pandas* (priests) on the *ghats* (banks) of Ganga which was only half an hour train journey from Gajraula.

I have a very good memory that goes as far back as 1945 when I was only three years old and we lived in a railway quarter in Bullandshehar. By all accounts I was a very naughty, intelligent, and creative little kid who loved to play all the time. I would sometimes play with Karuna, making her smile, even laugh. But my playmate was Binno. She and I played under the *kanher* trees that bore fragrant yellow flowers. We often covered our feet in yellow coloured soil, using water to make small castles. The soil was salty as we swallowed it, only to be later scolded by Amma. Amar, Hari, and Rajiv attended school. They often went to cinema, free, being sons of the railway babu. Binno and I were more often than not left at home. I used to complain to Baoji and he would give me a sweet smile, saying, "You are not old enough to understand films right now". Then, he would give me a one paisa coin with a large hole in the middle. I will wear the paisa coin on finger as a ring and run to the *Halwaai* (sweet vender) shop and ask for hot *jalebis*. I will get a *dauna* (a plate made of leaves) full of *jalebis* and share them with Binno and Amma, and then go out to play. This became almost a daily morning ritual.

When my father started drinking I do not know. Probably he did all his adult life. Babaji knew about it and so did Chachaji. They just accepted it as a bad habit. He tried to avoid drinking in presence of his father. But it became an addiction he could not control. He drank everyday, except on Tuesdays. When I was a teenager, he told me about his encounter with the famous singer, K. L. Saigal, when Baoji was posted at Allahabad. My father liked music and he was a big fan of Saigal. Baoji was well versed in Urdu, and also knew Farsi (Persian). Although he could read Hindi literature, he could not write in Hindi. He had a good command of the English language and wrote most of his letters in English to his sons, and in Urdu to some friends and relatives.

It so happened that Baoji was on night shift (4 pm to midnight) at the Allahabad railway station. Saigal was in Allahabad for shooting a film. He was staying at the railway guesthouse. Saigal was also well known for his excessive drinking. When Baoji learned about Saigal's presence, he could not resist his temptation to visit him at the guesthouse. He said to Saigal:

Saigal Sahib, I am a big fan of your singing. Your name is Kundan Lal (Saigal) and my name is also Kundan Lal (Sharma). You drink and I drink too. So why don't we have a mehfil (program) of your singing?

Saigal seemed reluctant initially, and said:

I can't play without the *peti* (harmonium).

Baoji arranged for the harmonium to be brought, as well as a bottle of imported whisky and meat *kababs*. Saigal was very pleased and sang for close to two hours. This was, for Baoji, one of the happiest moments of his life

2

HAPUR

Baoji was transferred to Hapur as a relieving assistant stationmaster in early 1946. As a relieving person, he could be assigned to any railway station within about a 75-kilometer radius. Hapur was a good-sized town and had a large railway colony. It was for Baoji his headquarter. We lived in a railway quarter which was small, with only two rooms, a verandah, a small kitchen, an open space about 15 feet by 15 feet and a toilet. There was a front door and a back door. A door that could be locked on either side connected the two rooms. The verandah was more than six feet wide, and with a strong chick drape, it worked as a large bedroom in which as many as four cots could be placed side to side for sleeping purposes. They were removed every morning to create open space. This is how a family of eight managed in a small railway quarter. Amma had a *chakki* (flour mill made of two heavy stones) where she ground *atta* (flour) every morning. She also had a *charkha* (spinning wheel) on which she spun cotton in her spare time. She also ground her own spices for use in cooking. She indeed was a hard working mother. There was no running water in the quarter. There was a common tap on the front of a row of quarters, and all the boys, and Binno, fetched water from that tap for household use. There was also no electricity in the quarters and we had to use lanterns with kerosene oil in every room at night.

Hapur had a high school and an intermediate college. It was also the second largest wheat *mandi* (wholesale market). Many railway stations in India were, and still are, famous for certain food item/snack/fruit: Nagpur for oranges; Allahabad for guavas; Sandila for *laddoos* (a round shaped sweet); Ghaziabad for *samosas* (a salty potato-filled pastry); Benaras for *langda aam* (a large size mango) and *paan* (betel leaf); Alwar for *kalakand* (a kind of milk cake); Khurja City for *khurchan* (a special sweet preparation made of milk); Aligarh for brass locks; Rewari for *rewaris* (a snack made of sesame seeds and sugar) Mathura for *peda* (a sweet made from milk); Kolkata for *rasgullas* (a well-known Bengali sweet made of milk cheese and sugar syrup; and Hapur for *papad* (a deep-fried round thin-layered snack made from potatoes). Hundreds of papad were sold to passengers in every train.

I felt like a free bird in Hapur. There was a large railway colony at this station. The station itself was large with two platforms connected by an underground passage. On the main platform was A. H. Wheeler bookshop that had all kinds of novels and it also sold newspapers and various magazines, in both Hindi and English. Right outside the railway station was a big covered area that had a number of shops that sold sweets, tea, and food. A rickshaw stand was right next door and perpendicular to that was the paved road that went towards the main town. Hapur had two movie theatres, Jaina Talkies and Shankar Talkies. There was a large vegetable market, and shops lined on both sides of the road. Not too far was a bus stand of Uttar Pradesh Public Transport where buses took passengers to nearby towns and cities, such as Meerut, Bijnor, Ghaziabad, Baghpat, and even Delhi. Hapur was a junction station on the Delhi-Moradabad line, but it also had the Meerut- Khurja line on which Bullandshehar was located.

Baoji was not always present in Hapur as he spent more time relieving other assistant stationmasters on different railway stations on both train lines. The nature of his relieving duty widened his social circle and he made numerous railway friends. Whenever he came home after out of station duty he would receive a report from Amma on all the children. In summer days, we took turns fanning him when he took an afternoon nap. Sometimes Baoji stayed in Hapur for several days until he was called on duty again. There was a Hindu *mandir* (temple) in the railway colony where we lived. Except for the three Muslim families almost everybody from Hindu families went to the temple each evening for *aarti* (ritualized group singing in the worship of Hindu gods). *Shankh* (conch shell) and *ghanti* (bells) were used alongside singing of *aarti*. This was followed by *prasad* where the temple priest will distribute *patashas* (sugar candies). This was the most favourite part of going to the *mandir* for little kids.

From mid-1946 to January 1948, I grew up to age 6. During this period I also became much naughtier, despite being the favourite son of my parents. I began to be trusted with all kinds of errands by Amma. I got into trouble many times, got hurt countless times and was mostly treated by my mother. On bleeding cuts and wounds she would apply a thin paste of *haldi* (turmeric) and *chuna* (white lime used in betel leaves). This paste had a fantastic medicinal quality. Healing was quite fast. I had a cot supported by two branches of an old *peepul* (a kind of poplar tree) tree, with its four legs hanging down at a height of about 10 feet above the ground. I used to lie down there on hot summer afternoons. It was a sort of "home away from home". Occasionally a friend from the neighbourhood would join me there to play a game of cards. I also played *gulli dandaa*, various ball games, games using *kanche* (marbles), and *ludo* (a board game), etc. One of my favourite pastimes was to look for empty cigarette packets on railway platforms and on rain tracks. I had quite a collection of cigarette packets: Wilson; Camel; Wills, Capstan; Red and White, Charminar, 555, Goldflake, and several other brands.

Baoji learned to eat meat in Hapur. Our next door neighbor with one common wall to our quarter was a Mr. Dalela, a permanent assistant stationmaster at the Hapur station. He was a Kayasth by caste, within the Kshatriya *varna*, one of the four broad divisions that are hierarchically arranged in the Hindu social order. And like most Kshatriyas, he ate meat quite regularly. He would often make fun of Baoji pertaining to Baoji's vegetarianism. Once he said: "Sharmaji, how can you eat grain with grain; *daal* (lentil) is grain and so is *gaihoon* (wheat) whose flour is used to make *chapatis?*". Baoji just ruefully smiled in response. One day Dalela sent a plate of mutton (lamb meat) for Baoji. Amma had a big fight with her husband on this issue. But Baoji wanted to try the dish. When Amma didn't allow her to eat it inside the house, Baoji took a small table and chair out of the house and ate it anyway. He obviously must have liked it. From then onwards, he would occasionally get a plate of the meat from a restaurant near the station. A Brahman became an occasional non-veg. Amma didn't like it a bit.

India became an independent country on August 15, 1947. We were in Hapur then. Initially, there was a lot of excitement and celebrating. We listened on the radio the message from Pandit Jawaharlal Nehru, independent India's first Prime Minister, a rather charismatic leader with socialist and liberal ideas. Unfortunately, along with the independence came the partition of the country, engineered by the last British Viceroy, Lord Mountbatten, Congress leaders and Muslim League leader, Mohammed Ali Jinnah. The country was divided into predominantly Hindu India and predominantly Muslim Pakistan, the latter consisting of two parts, West Pakistan in the west, and East Pakistan in the east, separated by over one thousand miles of India. The boundaries of the divisions were drawn rather arbitrarily, primarily along religious lines, with total disregard for cultural contiguity, including shared language, dress styles, dietary habits, and dress styles. Punjab in the west and Bengal on the east were sub-divided.

What the two newly formed countries witnessed was a mass exodus of historical proportions from both sides. Conservatively speaking, a few million people crossed border, Muslims from India going to either side of Pakistan, and Hindus from both East and West Pakistan crossing the border into India. People moved in a hurry, on foot, on bullock carts, in cars, buses, and trains. There was unprecedented violence: Hindus killed and raped Muslim women on their way to Pakistan; Muslims did the same to Hindus when they attempted to cross the border from Pakistan to India. Estimates vary, but very likely up to 2 million people lost lives. Those who succeeded to cross borders became refugees in the country they moved to.

Violence erupted in Hapur and the surrounding areas also. People who lived in the same communities in neighbourhoods, villages, and towns were split along communal lines. Trust disappeared and suspicion and hatred began to reign. There were many villages and towns around Hapur that had a large Muslim population, even a majority in some places. Hindus of Hapur, including those in the railway colony became fearful, some even paranoid. In the area where my family lived, the Hindus locked their houses, took their valuable possessions with them and went inside the *mandir* which was fortified with many obstacles placed inside at the main door entrance to deter a forced entry by the Muslim mob if they came. Baoji decided against moving to the temple and, as far as I can remember, ours was the only family in the colony that stayed put. The sense of fear was there, of course. But Baoji and Amma took out whatever weapons there were in the house. There was a sword, two daggers, a heavy wooden *laathi* (staff} that was used for killing snakes (a brass snake was nailed to it at the lower end), a *gandasa* (machete) that was used to prepare fodder for the cow, and a *daranti* (a tool used for cutting vegetables, consisting of a sharp curved blade attached to the wooden base). These were our weapons of defense in case of an attack by the Muslims. We also stole unburned coal from parked freight trains on the rail track, and burned them like a bonfire all night to keep guard. Members of the family took turns for the watch. We also made rather strong whips from electric wire wherever we found it. But the attack, luckily, never happened.

Mahatma Gandhi, the moral leader of the struggle for independence of India from British colonialism, who was against India's partition but was outvoted by other Congress party leaders, was assassinated on January 30, 1948 near Birla Mandir in New Delhi when he was going for his evening prayers. A man called Nathu Ram Godse, a right wing Hindu fundamentalist, shot him. The nation was in a shock. Although cremated near the river Yamuna in Delhi, a special train from Delhi to Hardwar transported his ashes. Hapur was on the train's route. That was also the day when Baoji was transferred to Gajraula. There were hundreds of thousands of people who came to the railway platform in Hapur to pay their respects. The train that was to take us from Hapur to Gajraula was delayed by several hours and we arrived in Gajraula way past midnight on a rather chilly February night in 1948.

3

GAJRAULA

Gajraula was a neat little town, much smaller than Hapur. It was also a junction, as there was a railway line going from Gajraula to Bijnor. But the station only had one platform. Baoji was now assistant stationmaster in Gajraula. He was posted there, so he did not have to relieve anybody at other stations. Amar did his high school in Hapur and one year of his intermediate college in Hapur before the transfer to Gajraula. He completed his second year there as well while he stayed with a friend for one year in a village near Hapur. Hari did grade nine in Hapur and Rajiv did grade seven.. Soon, at the beginning of the next school year, Baoji sent Hari and Rajiv to Rewari to study there while staying with Ram Kumar Chachaji. There was only a primary school in Gajraula. Binno, Karuna, and I stayed with Baoji and Amma, and we were home schooled by the older brothers whenever they came to Gajraula to visit.

I learned to play carom board with new friends in Gajraula. My brothers taught me several games of playing cards, especially rummy and flash (three-card poker). I soon became a smart rummy player. Being the only male child living with the parents for a change, I cultivated a feeling of being important to the family as well as to my two sisters. I was not spoiled but I certainly received more attention and concern from both Baoji and Amma. Although there were railway porters to do jobs like fetching water or buy things from the market, I was trusted with making shopping lists, even keeping accounts. Like Baoji, Amma was very religious too. They both did their *puja* every day. Amma will keep fasts on many days during the year, such as *Ram Naumi* (Ram's birthday), *Janamashtami* (Krishna's birthday), *Shiv Ratri* (Shiv's birthday), *Karva Chauth* (a fast most women in north India kept for the wellbeing and longevity of their husband), in addition to every Monday. For a sort of periodic ritual cleansing, Amma and Baoji held Satya Narayan Katha when friends and neighbours were invited and offered *prasad* at the end of the Katha. All of the children and Baoji fasted on Ram Navmi, Janamashtami and Shiv Ratri. Baoji also fasted every Tuesday for his deity, Hanuman. He always abstained from drinking on this day each week. Every beggar who came to the door was given something, a Roti, some grain, or a few coins. On Saturdays a man would come and would take copper coins and mustard oil to ward off the family from evil spirits. Some days were good for travel, others not. Tuesday was considered an auspicious day and most important undertakings were initiated on this day. There was a strong belief in astrology and every member of the family had a *janam patri* (horoscope). Thus ritual and belief dictated life and gave people strength to carry on with their lives.

On most railway stations there was one stationmaster and two assistant stationmasters. All three performed 8 hours of duty each day. The shifts were from 8 am to 4 pm, 4 pm to midnight, and midnight to 8 am. The stationmaster always took the day shift. The assistant stationmasters performed the two night shifts. Baoji would be on duty from 4 pm to midnight, or from midnight to 8 am. These shifts changed on a weekly or monthly basis, negotiated by the two ASMs under the guidance and approval of the SM. During the evening shift, Baoji would come home for supper or his supper would be taken to him to his office. During the night shift he would have a late supper and then come home for breakfast the next morning. While he would be on night shifts, he would take long naps during the day as he was unable to sleep in the evening before his midnight shift. When he came back from his 4 pm to midnight shift, he would water the garden in front of the quarter that had several papaya trees, and vegetable plants such as okra, *lauki* (a long squash), tomatoes, beans, carrots, *methi*, radish, *palak* (spinach), and *dhania* (coriander). He took great pride in his garden. Amma would go in the garden only to pick the produce.

There was a significant day in Gajraula that I especially remember. One afternoon Baoji had just completed his afternoon siesta to ready his body clock for a late night duty. During the several days before, Baoji had casually mentioned to Amma more than once that during the night he had felt something crawl over his feet in the garden while he was watering the plants with the hose. Amma had brushed the observation aside, saying that he was simply imagining things. Well, it turned out that there was some substance to Baoji's thinking. One autumn afternoon In Gajraula, Baoji was relaxing on a muddha (bamboo chair). A whole bunch of kids were playing nearby, my two sisters and I being among them. Suddenly we heard the melodious sound of snake charmer's *been* (flute). He was playing a popular film tune. He came close to Baoji and said to him, "Sir, there is a poisonous snake in your garden, a cobra; very dangerous. If you wish, I can take it out of the garden. But it will cost you".

Baoji thought the *sanpera* was kidding and expressed that view to him. But apparently the snake charmer was not kidding. He retorted by saying:

"I will show you".

"How much would you charge?"

'Two rupees for milk to feed the snake and a *lungi*."

Reluctantly Baoji agreed. The snake charmer put down the snake baskets connected by a wooden *lathi*. He took the money and lungi up front. He sat down on the ground. And started playing his been again. He played the flute for about four to five minutes, stopped playing, made promises to the snake: "I will not break your teeth. I won't take your poison glands out, and will feed you milk." He then drew a circle on the ground with the non-playing end of his flute, and repeated the promises again to the snake. By now a big crowd had gathered in front of our living quarter. The kids were scared, and I thought the adults were too. The snake charmer started to count, "*Ek, Do Teen,* and *Sadhe Teen*" (one, two, three, three and a half). The moment he said "*sadhe teen*", a large black cobra appeared from nowhere and jumped to the centre of the circle. Everyone moved a few feet back, with intrigue, fear, and amazement. The snake charmer played the flute some more, and gradually and stealthily grabbed the snake with his hands in a flash and with amazing speed transferred it to one of the baskets.

Even Baoji became convinced and stared at Amma, saying, "I told you that there was a snake in the garden but you wouldn't believe me"

The intrigue was not over yet. The snake charmer said to my father: "There is another snake in your garden. The other one is the female, the partner of the one I just caught. If I do not take the other one out too, it will seek revenge."

Baoji said. "You think we are fools?"

"How dare I think that sahib? But what I told you is the truth. Should I take her out too?"

Baoji said, "Yes." The snake charmer demanded the same amount for the other snake, received it, went through the same routine, and out came the second, almost identical looking snake. He put it in the basket too. After a few more minutes he walked away.

The memory of this intrigue-filled afternoon has been etched in my memory ever since. I became fascinated with snakes for as long as I lived in India after that episode. I encountered many and I also killed a few.

With the absence of a regular school, and none of Binno, Karuna, and myself getting a formal education, Gajraula provided us with happy time. Of course, Baoji continued to drink every evening, and there were frequent outbursts by him while drunk, but he was sober as a saint during daytime. During his outbursts, Amma was not the one to keep calm. She gave back as much as she received, orally of course. Baoji decided to send Binno and me to a Sanskrit school. But that didn't last long, The teacher was a middle aged Brahmin who, like my father, kept a *choti*, but he covered his head with a white Gandhi *topi* (cap). Being naughty as usual, one day I crossed the limit. The class was conducted on a *chabutra* (concrete platform) surrounding a large *peepul* tree. What I did was pre-planned. I carried from home a thin rope at the end of which was attached a metal hook. Before the class began that day, I had already climbed the tree and found a spot exactly above where the teacher sat. As soon as the class began, I started to drop the rope with the hook at the bottom. On my third attempt I was able to pluck the *topi* (cap) right off the head of the teacher. At first, he didn't know what was happening, but when the kids started laughing and looking upwards at the tree, the teacher looked up too. Finding me up there with his *topi*, he yelled at me really hard and ordered me to come down at that very instant. Scared that he might beat me up, I came down with my eyes lowered, guilty as one can be. I was spared the beating, but he ordered me to get out from the class. The report of the episode reached Baoji; he too was angry and yelled at me. That was the end of the adventure of learning at the Sanskrit school.

While we were in Gajraula, the oldest brother, Amar, was in Meerut, attending Meerut College for his B.A. degree. He stayed in the hostel of the college for two years, coming home only for holidays. While in the college he got in the habit of gambling, which became a problem without him realizing this. He will lose money meant for tuition and living expenses in the card game and would be forced to borrow. Once I was sent by Baoji to Meerut with the final university exam fee for Amar. I stayed in Meerut for a few days and saw the lifestyle of Amar. He lost all his money in the game of cards, had to borrow to play one last hand in which he, luckily, recovered his loss.

Before his final examination, pressure was put on Amar to get married. It was actually my Babaji's (paternal grandfather's) insistence that Amar marry. He was only seventeen, and the girl who he was destined to marry was only 15. She came from Ajmer, had lost both her parents at a young age, and was brought up by her uncle and his wife. The uncle was a man of modest means and was in no position to spend lavishly on the wedding. It was a simple marriage. The *baraat* came from Gajraula where all the relatives had assembled a week before the wedding. Amar's marriage festivities were fun time for all and sundry. The youngsters of my age and up ate a lot, chased the pretty girls in the area, and ate all the sweets they could at the *Halwaai's* shop on credit. The bill was settled by Baoji later and he was shocked in horror with the amount owed to the sweet shop. Before the marriage, the younger folk made a trip by train to Bridge Halt station to take a dip in the Ganga River. That was a fun-filled trip.. On the trees-lined walk from the train station to the river *ghats* (banks) there were a lot of red-faced monkeys, looking for food. There were countless hard-shelled turtles in the Ganga river. We spent several hours lying in the river water, and then had a meal consisting of *Puris* (fried bread), *Aloo* (dry potato curry), and *Halwa* (a sweet dish made out of *Suji* flour). After a sumptuous meal, some had a siesta while others played cards, even gambled, before taking the return train to Gajraula in the evening.

Ajmer was far away from Gajraula and the train journey took two days for the *baraat* to reach Ajmer. The *baraat* consisting of more than a hundred people, was accommodated in a *Dharamshala* (a rather modest building made from charity funds). All members of the *baraat* had brought their own bedding in holdalls. All members of my immediately family were dressed in brand new clothes tailored especially for the occasion. The members of the *baraat* were served meals, tea, and snacks right at the *Dharamshala*. We were taken to the bride's house for special ceremonies only. On one of the ceremonial occasions when the young baraatis were sitting on chairs on the main floor of the house.,the friends of the bride were giggling and making quite a raucous upstairs. Then we were all treated to a nasty surprise. Mustard oil was poured onto to our new and attractive bush-shirts. Our shoes were also stolen and were not given back to us until we had to give money to the satisfaction of the miscreants.

The marriage of Amar, on April 20, 1950, was overall a generally happy event. The baraat returned to Gajraula along with the bride. Many members of the baraat got off earlier, where they lived or closer to their abodes. I first talked to my bhabhi (sister-in-law) on this return journey. She was a very pretty and sweet 15-year old young woman, who called me "bhayya", meaning brother. I knew ours was going to be a lifelong relationship based upon mutual respect and affection. Bhabhi returned to Ajmer a few days later and Amar left for Meerut for his final B.A. degree examination. Life in Gajraula returned to normal, post-marriage. But not for too long.

Baoji had hemorrhoids that bled frequently. He did not want to discuss his condition with most people. But it was a painful condition. The doctors, in both Gajraula and Moradabad (the divisional headquarter), had advised surgery, but Baoji kept postponing it. He was afraid of the knife. He had never had surgery in his life. He was also afraid of the needles. But now the condition demanded that he had to have surgery. A date for surgery was fixed in May of 1950. Amma decided to accompany Baoji to Moradabad and took me along as well. It was to be a major surgery under general anaesthesia. Amma and I stayed at Baoji's friend's house. The operation went well but it required a long healing time. Baoji stayed at the Moradabad railway hospital for two weeks before he was discharged. He did not like the food at the hospital. So, Amma cooked food for him at the friend's house and took it to the hospital.

This was my first visit to Moradabad. I was excited to be in the large town that was known for its brass and silver work. Amma and I went to the market one day and bought a brass *paandaan* (a beetle leaf box with sections for leaves, liquid lime, *Kattha, supari,* chewing tobacco and other condiments) for Baoji. We were sure that this *paandaan* would make Baoji very happy. And it did, as we later found out. Two weeks after Baoji's surgery, we brought him home to Gajraula. He required one more month to fully recover. During all this time he was not allowed to drink. To put it mildly, Baoji was a difficult man during this ordeal.

4

UMARTALI

As soon as Baoji had fully got his health back, he started drinking. It was the same old Baoji once again. And, suddenly, out of the blue, he got his transfer order. No one in the family was sure whether to be happy or sad. Baoji was getting a promotion as stationmaster. But Umartali was a very small railway station on the main Moradabad-Lucknow railway line. Situated in Hardoi district, it was one station away from Sandila, the railway station known for its *laddoos* that were sold in earthen pots covered by a thin red paper that was attached to the pot by a small piece of *sutli* (string). Lucknow was only 25 miles to the east of Umartali. Only the passenger trains stopped at Umartali. Express and mail trains would zoom by at a high speed.

We were transferred to Umartali on a hot summer day in May, the temperature high at 30 C even in the evening. Our railway quarter was much bigger than the one in Gajraula. Next to the living quarter, was a very large garden, almost half an acre in size. The previous stationmaster was a Muslim who had a great love for gardens. There were several dozens of mature fruit bearing trees: mango, guava, orange, *jamun*, apple, pear, papaya, loquat, plum, peach, kino, *bel patra*, mausmi, grapes, and nectarine. The fruit garden was fenced on all four sides. The fence was six foot high and was made of heavy mesh wire. On this fence ran the creeping plants of zucchini, which were loaded with the vegetable in season. There was a large peepul tree next to the quarter and several neem trees that provided shade from the hot sun. We were all excited about the garden. None more than Baoji and Amma.

There were two large cement benches at the back of the house. Next to the fruit garden was a cornfield, with a much lower fence surrounding it. The stationmaster's office was about 3 to 4 minutes walk from the living quarter. There was no electricity in Umartali and no running water. The railway porters supplied the water for household use from a well nearby. Despite Umartali being a small station, Baoji was very happy there. He was the "king" of the railway station, its almighty CEO, with two assistant stationmasters who worked the night shifts, two signal porters on each side of the railway platform, a general purpose porter named Maikoo, and a sweeper who kept the platform and the railway station's office clean, and cleaned the latrines of the railway quarters. Everyone was dependent on Maikoo who ran all sorts of errands for Amma and the kids, aside from his other duties at the railway station. Binno, Karuna, and I had a carefree life in Umartali. No school to attend. We were tutored at home by Baoji and by three older brothers who came home for summer months.

After his graduation from Meerut College, Amar came home to Umartali, hoping that he would find a job in the near future. Hari and Rajeev were studying in Rewari where they lived with Chachaji and Chachi. Amar's wife, Sanyukta, came to Umartali on a permanent basis after the *gauna* ceremony when the dowry accompanies the bride and the marriage is consummated. Amma taught Sanyukta Bhabhi the art of cooking and the latter assumed much of the kitchen responsibility. Every three to four months Bhabhi visited Ajmer to be with her family.

Soon after Amar came to Umartali he came down with tuberculosis. Amma had lost both her brothers to tuberculosis many years earlier. Both she and Baoji were worried about Amar. He was under the care of a railway doctor in Moradabad. A railway doctor in Hardoi also saw him. The family also had to worry about their own health, as TB is infectious. Amar was also prohibited from having any physical relationship with Bhabhi until he was fully cured of TB. Amar started to do painting. At this time his medium was water colour. He started with a painting he copied from the well-known Bengali artist Uma Vakil. The painting depicted Krishna, Radha, and a number of Gopis, along with a cow. Krishna was shown playing his flute. Amar gave 52 washes to this painting before it was completed. The whole family along with Amar were very happy with the painting. It was framed in glass.

Amar was creative with his hands. He built a chess set with all the counters made in clay. I learned the game of chess when I was only 9 years old. My *Mausaji* (Amma's sister's husband), Mool Chand, taught me the game and I became pretty good at it at a very young age. During the hot summer months of 1950 and 1951, I visited Rampur Katra, a village where *Mausaji* lived. He was a very rich man with many servants and a large house in the village. He owned a lot of land, had a very big orchard of Dusheri aams (mangoes), a very popular mango variety. With no kids of their own—their only child, a daughter named Sharbati having died at age 13—Mausaji and Mausi (named Jadawali), became close and attached to the children of Tika Ram, Mool Chand's younger brother. Tika Ram was a business savvy man. The two brothers were into cotton business and exported it to several countries around the world. They had a large team of weavers and dyers in Rampur Katra. Mool Chand Mausaji had a large collection of religious books, including the Gita and the epic poems Ramayan and Mahabharat. I read them both with unbridled enthusiasm and did so in quick time. Mool Chand *Mausaji* had a temper, but he was kind and affectionate to the kids. For some reason I became his favourite among the kids. He taught me a lot of things that I still remember.

Jadawali *Mausi* was older than Amma by three years. She became attached to my older sister, Binno, and wanted to bring her to her extended family as the bride of Tika Ram's middle son, Nand Kishore. But that did not happen; Binno eventually became the bride of the youngest son of Tika Ram, named Shiv Kumar. He was five years older than me, but despite the age difference, Shiv Kumar and I became buddies. We used to roast the freshly dug potatoes from their field in the slow-burning dung fire. The potatoes tasted yummy. Nand Kishore ran a shop in Barabanki, and the oldest, Ghan Shyam, another shop in Gorakhpur. Binno, Karuna and I became frequent visitors to Barabanki and Rampur Katra during the early 1950s. Shiv Kumar was the consummate farmer and, living in Rampur Katra, he took care of the land and the mango orchard. In 1954 he became my brother-in-law, marrying Binno when she was only 15 and he himself only 17.

Back in Umartali, I began to publicly recite Ramayana, and cultivated an audience from the surrounding area. Both Amma and Baoji liked that enormously. Baoji took interest in my studies and taught me how to read and write Urdu. He used to get the Urdu daily newspapers, Milaap and Partaap. We also received Pioneer from Lucknow and The Hindustan Times, also the Lucknow edition of Statesman. Baoji was thus well read and well informed. For a mere High School graduate, this was an amazing feat, certainly most unusual. He inculcated this quest for knowledge in all his sons.

During the summer of 1951, Hari came home from Alwar where he had moved from Rewari to live on his own. In order to make ends meet, he had to sell his bicycle. Baoji was very mad at Hari and scolded him. Hari went back to Alwar and he started working as a typist in a lawyer's office. In his spare time. he also wrote or typed letters for people to make extra money, at the rate of one anna per letter. An anna was one-sixteenth of a rupee. Of all my brothers, I had a special bonding with Hari. He loved me a lot, and, being closer to Baoji, I served to protect him from Baoji's anger. Hari used to play the flute. Curiously, on his trips out in the fields for natural calls, he would sit down near a snake hole and play the flute, hoping that he would draw the snake out. But, of course, that never happened.

Finally, after a long wait, Amar found a job as teacher of art in a small rural school, in a village called Meetli, near Baghpat in western Uttar

Pradesh. Everyone was excited and happy in the family, none more than Baoji. Baoji forced Amar to take me with him so that I could start school. Amar had no choice in the matter and he reluctantly agreed. Bhabhi was still in Ajmer.

From Umartali we took the passenger train to Sandila, and then Sealdah Express from Sandila and got off the train at a station called Shahdara just before Delhi, which was a junction as a narrow gage line went from Shahdara to Saharanpur. We got off at a train station called Baghpat, which was a small town, predominantly inhabited by members of the Jat caste. From Baghpat we took a rickshaw to the village of Meetli. The landscape consisted of agricultural fields. There were fields of sugar cane, maize, *jowar*, tomatoes, *tinda*, *lauki*, and other vegetables. The school had arranged for Amar and me to stay with the rich Jat landlord of the village. A Brahman widow, the mother of a boy my age, named Ram Singh, was to cook meals for us. For a nine year old I had a voracious appetite; I probably ate more than Amar. Those were generally happy days for me. Going to school for the first time was a great experience. I began to feel that most of what I was being taught at school I knew already through home schooling. But going over the same material was not bad.

Hari visited us once in Meetli. That was a great time. We played a game of field hockey with the other boys that I liked very much. But after Hari left, I began to feel miserable, especially on weekends when Amar would leave on Friday after school for Delhi to be with his friends there. I used to cry of loneliness. On one Saturday late afternoon, Baoji suddenly arrived in Meetli. As soon as I saw Baoji, I started crying. Baoji got very angry with Amar. In the Jat landlord he found a drinking companion. The two drank a lot. The alcohol caused Baoji lose all his inhibitions. He yelled loudly at Amar, called him a lot of swear words, and he ordered me to pack up to go back to Umartali the next day. I believe that was the beginning of an emotional divide between Baoji and Amar, his oldest living son.

Baoji and I returned to Umartali the next day. It was once again back to the carefree days of no school for me and spending a lot of time with my two sisters. Baoji started consuming a larger quantity of country liquor everyday, and having heated arguments with Amma where he would express his anger over, and disappointment in, Amar. This would become an enduring routine and pattern with him for the rest of his life. He started to think seriously about finding a way to move to a larger train station with schools so that his youngest three kids could get a formal school education that had been impossible until then.

One night during his drinking session, Baoji asked for his reading glasses, a pen and a postcard, He suddenly had the urge for writing a letter to his younger brother, Ram Kumar Chachaji. He wanted to thank him for putting up Hari and Rajeev and putting them through high school and Hari through high school and intermediate college. He started writing in his nice handwriting:

"My dear Ram Kumar, my dear brother, my dearest brother….". He could not write anymore. He finished that letter the next morning before gong on duty. He also wanted me to write another letter in Hindi (which he could not), this one to Ganpat Bhai Sahib, Amma's deceased brother's son. His full name was Ganpat Rai Swami and he was a contractor for installing water taps in the town of Alwar where he lived with his family that consisted of several children. His oldest child, a son named Radhey Shyam, was my age, just six months younger than me. In terms of kinship and generational relationship, Ganpat Rai was my cousin (my mother's brother's son) and Radhey Shyam was my nephew. But Radhey Shyam and I became great buddies.

After Ganpat Rai left for Alwar, Radhey stayed back in Umartali. Now I had a male playmate. Both of us were naughty and often landed up in trouble. Radhey Shyam stayed in Umartali for over two months. The two of us decided to make bows and arrows. We searched for raw material that was not difficult to find. A long weed near puddles of water provided ideal material to make arrows. We searched for flat thin pieces of tin to make arrowheads. We split one end of arrows to a very small length, we fastened the tin to the arrows with melted shellac, which was made available to us by Maikoo. Now we were totally ready to become hunters of small targets. We killed a few birds.

One day, around mid morning Baoji was getting a shave from the barber. Baoji was in bad mood whenever he got a shave. It was one of those days. Radhey Shyam and I had had our breakfast and had even studied for a while. Now it was time for some fun and frolic. We took out our bows and arrows. I aimed the arrow at a bird on a pomegranate tree of which we had three in the garden. I missed my target and the arrow got stuck on a high branch on the tree. I was desperate to get my arrow back. Radhey Shyam lent me his back so that I could reach the arrow. Pomegranate branches are delicate and this one was loaded with fruit. I put some pressure to bend the branch to reach the arrow. The branch broke off with all the fruits on it.

Amma saw the broken branch with all the small, not quite ripe, fruits. She complained to Baoji about our actions. Baoji, already in an angry mood with the barber who had cut him at two or three places while shaving, got totally ballistic and started hitting both Radhey Shyam and me, but I soon became the sole target of his anger. He hit me and hit me hard, with his hands, shoes or whatever else came in his hands. I had never seen Baoji in that way. Even Amma was shocked with the thrashing I had received. Having initially provoked his anger by complaining, now she tried to shield me from Baoji's brutality. He stopped beating me only when he himself got tired. I was in rough shape with his punches, black and blue all over the body. I was crying loudly.

Amma felt very guilty and applied medicines over my body. She also gave me hot milk with turmeric. By nightfall Baoji was totally calm. He apologized to me: "Beta, sorry I got carried away. Does it hurt a lot?" He summoned Maikoo and sent him to Sandila to get some *laddoos* and hot *jalebis* for Radhey Shyam and especially me. My hurt didn't pain all that much, and my body marks healed in a few days. That was the first and the only time my father had hit me. He never did it again. Ironically, he wasn't even drunk when he did that.

5

HAPUR AGAIN

In March of 1952 Baoji was transferred again to Hapur. He had worked very hard for this transfer, even though he was to become Relieving Station Master. He did not get a railway quarter for quite some time. Initially we had to put all our household belongings in a rather dilapidated and awkward looking two-room place. The family spent more than two weeks living in a huge circular one- room place with a high ceiling, which was also inhabited by a large number of pigeons. That is the reason why Amma used to sarcastically call it a *"Kabutarkhana"* (a place resided by pigeons). The room was full of pigeon droppings. Obviously, Amma was not at all happy with the arrangement. After a lot of running around, Baoji was able to find a rental accommodation some distance away from the train station. It was a decent place with two rooms, a large verandah one side of which also served as the kitchen, a latrine, and a small room serving as the bathroom. This place of residence was on the first floor, and the railway authorities paid the rent.

Across the road was a big house with a huge garden and a circular driveway. The railway overseer and his family lived in this bungalow. The lawn of this bungalow was beautifully maintained. The boys in the area played cricket on this lawn. This was my first introduction to the game. I was 10 years old. I made friends with the boys and joined them in the game. A set of bricks was used to make wickets. A local carpenter made cheap and crude bats and we used a cloth ball stuffed with tightly packed rags and sewn by a leather needle by the shoe repairman.

Soon I got very sick. I had high temperature, going as high as 106 F and I could not eat or drink anything. The temperature will go up and come down. I was taken to the railway doctor who thought I had malaria and gave me medication for it. Baoji was away on relieving duty. In fact, after his transfer to Hapur this time around, we did not see much of him. He returned home one evening and saw me burning with high fever. I had not passed urine for two days. Amma had been putting a piece of cloth soaked in cold water on my forehead almost constantly. But to no avail. My father immediately summoned a private doctor whom he had to pay a lot of money, 50 rupees, to make the house call. The doctor said, "Your son does not have malaria. He has typhoid". He prescribed penicillin tablets to me. Penicillin was just then introduced as a new medicine, a very potent antibiotic that saved millions of lives globally. The doctors helped me pass urine through insertion of a tube in my penis. I passed two large containers full of urine. Soon my swelling and fever came down. I was on the antibiotic for a week. But one has to be very careful with diet when you are inflicted with typhoid.

Bhabhi came to Hapur. Everybody, even Amma, went out to see a cinema. Bhabhi and I were alone in the house. She was cooking *chapatis*. I had not eaten anything solid for over three weeks. I begged Bhabhi to give me a chapatti. She most reluctantly gave me a chapatti to eat. It was so nice to eat solid food after so many days. I rinsed my mouth and fell asleep. By the time others returned from the movie, my fever had returned and it went high again. I had a relapse of typhoid. Amma was so mad: *"aye chhori, tune jara bhi akal nahi. Kyon di roti use."* (Hey girl, you have no brains! Why did you give him a chapatti?). I had to fight typhoid again for two more weeks. This time Karuna also came down with typhoid and had to be put on penicillin. It took the two of us four weeks to fully recover. We became very dark, and our scalps were full of dirt and muck. I had not had a bath in seven weeks, and Karuna for four weeks. Baoji brought a barber home. A sharp razor knife shaved Karuna's and my heads. We both had passed through a great ordeal.

During my sickness, our house was full. Amar and Sanyukta Bhabhi were visiting from Delhi where Amar had found a job teaching art at DAV Higher Secondary School in Paharganj. He was subletting a room from a government employee living on Minto Road in New Delhi, very close to Cannaught Place. Ram Kumar Chachaji, Chachi, and Rajeev came from Rewari, and Hari was visiting from Alwar. The house was indeed full. But it was summer time and everyone slept under the open sky on cots. Soon everyone, except Rajeev, left. He was to study in the intermediate college. I was to attend the school for the first time, except for the brief Meetli outing.

Baoji took me to Commercial and Industrial High School and Intermediate College in Hapur for admission. I was subjected to rigorous testing in every subject. I was well taught at home. The school admitted me into grade 8. I was only 10 years old. Thus started a new chapter in my life, one based upon institutionalized education. Karuna was admitted in grade four. Amma decided against sending Binno to school. In the back of her head, she was planning Binno's marriage with Shiv Kumar as soon as it was possible. That was also the wish of my Babaji (father's father). Soon after we were all admitted, Baoji finally got a railway quarter close to the Hapur railway station. It was a much better accommodation close to trains, doctor, shops, sweets, the noise of trains and passengers. The school was more than a kilometer away. It was an Arya Samaj (based on Vedanta philosophy) school, and all students were required to come before 6 o'clock in the morning. We were required to partake in daily *yagya* (worship with offering to the fire in a square box) and *pooja* for almost a whole hour. I learned the Gayatri Mantra by heart. This was followed by physical instruction and finally the classes would start at around 8 am. The school ended at 1 pm. Then those who played sports stayed back. I was one of them. I played cricket and field hockey. After reaching home, I would have a snack, do my homework quickly, and then would be anxious to play again.

The adults on the railway staff used to play volleyball everyday close to the railway station. Initially I used to watch them play. Occasionally, they would bring me in and hit some balls when someone needed a break. Within a month I became a permanent fixture of the volleyball playing personnel. I learned the game quickly, especially serving. I was generally appreciated as a player. Baoji used to hear about my volleyball playing and was appreciative. As long as my studies were not compromised, he would allow me to do anything. I also became the errand boy for the family. I was often sent to buy vegetables and grocery. I was also asked to write letters.

Whenever Baoji was on duty at a railway station not too far away from Hapur, Amma will cook his food, pack it in a tiffin carrier, and it was my duty to go to the railway station, wait for the train's arrival, and give the tiffin carrier to the guard of the caboose. I was also required to pick up the empty tiffin carrier. I rather enjoyed doing this as people on the railway station began to know him. I began to spend a good deal of time on the railway platform, especially near the A. H. Wheeler Bookstore. They came to know me well and they would let me borrow books, novels, and magazines from them for reading right on the railway platform and then returning back to them. One particular genre of novels I began to like were detective novels of which I must have read several hundred during the three years from 1952 to 1955.

One day, at the Hapur railway platform, while I was waiting for the train's arrival to deliver Baoji's tiffin carrier to the guard of the caboose, I noticed a huge crowd. Upon inquiry, I was told that Prithviraj Kapur's theatre troupe was traveling by the oncoming train from Delhi to go to Haridwar where the troupe was to perform in theatres. As the train stopped, all the actors got off to say hello to their fans. Prithvi Raj Kapur was a big burly man, wearing a white kurta (with chest buttons open) and pajama. He was accompanied by his youngest son, Shashi Kapur and his grandsons (Raj Kapur's sons), Randhir Kapur and Rishi Kapur. All three of them were wearing shorts and shirt. I made my way to the stars and requested

Prithviraj for an autograph. He looked at me with smiling eyes, wrote his first name Prithvi in Hindi and handed it over to me, saying *"Leejiye"* (here it is). I was so thrilled I forgot about the tiffin carrier and Baoji's food. As the train started leaving the platform, I ran to the Caboose and was barely able to hand over the tiffin carrier to the guard.

Baoji was a simply dressed man. He received sets of winter and summer uniforms from the Northern Railway's Moradabad division. The railway tailors knew his size. For summer uniform he was given white cotton pair of pants and jackets made in the style of Nehru jackets. For winter uniform he received black heavy woolen pair of pants and jackets. Baoji did not like to wear the uniform pants, even in the cold winter months. He was a cotton pajama man. Whenever he got new sets of uniform, he would ask Amma to get the pants altered from the tailor to fit Rajeev and, later, me. I remember one summer day in Hapur in 1954. Nehru was the prime minister of India at that time and Lal Bahadur Shastri was the Railway Minister in Nehru's cabinet. That day Shastri was on an inspection tour of the Northern Railway. When the train that carried him stopped at Hapur station he was respectfully greeted by Baoji who happened to be on relieving duty at the Hapur railway station. Shastri was a very short man, barely five feet tall. My father, at 6 feet one inch towered over him. Baoji was wearing his white uniform jacket with the Station Master emblem pinned on it and a pair of white cotton pajama. When Shastri noticed Baoji without his uniform pants, he raised his eyebrows and asked Baoji in Hindi: *"Are bade babu, aapki patloon kahan hai?"* (Hey, Mr. Stationmaster, where is your uniform pant?). Baoji felt embarrassed and had a wry smile on his face. He responded: "Sir, *yeh darzi log mere size ki patloon banate hi nahi theek se*" ("Sir, the tailors always make a mistake on my pants' size"). There was a loud blast of laughter by both.

Rajeev had his own set of friends and social network. He too was very smart and excelled in his studies. Being on relieving duty, Baoji became even more independent in his lifestyle, in the type of friends he made, and new habits he acquired. He started smoking *charas* (a form of cannibas) that he would ask me or Rajeev to buy for him from the market. This was a new habit and it made him a bit high even during the daytime when he did not drink alcohol. He also began to eat meat more frequently, ordering it from a restaurant near the railway station. All of this created more rift between him and Amma and his older sons. But his wish always prevailed. Needless to say, he became increasingly difficult to deal with.

I saw my first film in Hapur in 1952. It was *Humlog*, starring Balraj Sahani and Nutan. I liked it a lot. My next one was *Albela*, starring Geeta Bali and Bhagwan. Baoji was not a big film fan but he did go to see a film occasionally, sometimes with only Amma, and occasionally with the whole family. Watching films became a habit for me without compromising my studies. During a month I could see as many as three or four movies, Baoji gave the money for the films. Those days, cinema tickets cost, on a student concession rate, seven and a half *annas*, a little less than half a rupee. I was doing well at school. I was good in languages, both Hindi and English, I was considered brilliant in mathematics (arithmetic, algebra, and geometry) and science, I loved history, and my general knowledge was at the level of house school graduates. I made many friends at school, both boys and girls. My closest friend was Buddh Prakash Sharma, whose nickname was Buddhi. We stayed friends for many years.

Amar was doing well in Delhi. He had joined Delhi Polytechnic as a part-time student to do a national diploma in Fine Arts. It took him seven years to do that. He had a bicycle, which he used to go to teach at the D.A.V. Higher Secondary School in Pahar Ganj. He moved out of Minto Road sublet in 1952 to a *barsaati* (one room bachelor pad) in Karol Bagh. He would come home after teaching the morning shift, rest for some time, and then go for his polytechnic classes at Kashmiri Gate in the evening. Amar was very fond of watching movies too. He saw *Jhanak Jhanak Payal Baaje* about 40 times. At the same time he was a very hardworking, driven and focused individual. Nothing seemed to bother him and his work. As time went on, he did a lot for his family, especially his brothers and younger sister. At the same time, he demanded fierce loyalty, respect, and submission from all who lived with him. Rajeev was accepted in the bachelor of architecture degree program at Delhi Polytechnic in 1954 after completing his F.Sc. with first division standing in Hapur. He started living with Amar and Bhabhi in Karol Bagh. Baoji was helpless in this matter and began to feel the first dent in his patriarchal authority.

6

BINNO'S MARRIAGE

Jadawali Mausi and Amma's combined efforts culminated in the fixing of a date for Binno and Shiv Kumar's marriage. The Brahman priest was consulted and the muhurat (auspicious date and time) was for the early hours of December 4, 1954. Amma worked very hard for the marriage, gradually buying and accumulating items for the dowry: saris, jewelery, bed, other furniture, and miscellaneous items for siblings and other relatives of the groom. Baoji and Amma had started saving for Binno's wedding soon after Amar's marriage. It had been over four years since Amar was married. As for Binno herself, it was hard to understand if she was happy or sad about her forthcoming marriage. After all, she was still a child, born on January 30, 1939. Once she asked me: "Why are they marrying me so early? Why can't I go to school like you and Karuna?" I did not know how to respond to her. I was three years her junior and in matters as serious as marriage we had no say. However, I felt that she was getting a raw deal by getting married so early. Binno was not Amma's favourite. She was made to work hard. She wanted Binno to be the best she could be in household chores. Many a times Binno was physically punished by Amma. But Baoji never showed any dislike for Binno. In his eyes she was his daughter and worthy of equal love and care. Given Amma's indifference towards Binno,. it would not have been surprising for my sister to dream about a different lifestyle in a new family.

Preparations for the marriage went in high gear. Rajeev and I worked hard for some of the arrangements as Baoji was not always in Hapur. But one could see the pride in his eyes, the pride of a father of the bride to be. However, this did not prevent him from being difficult. In fact, his drinking became heavier and his behaviour more erratic and unpredictable. His fights with Amma also became more menacing, usually only verbally, but occasionally also physically. Once he hit Rajeev very hard who was trying to shield Amma from his physical assault. He became violent and suicidal. Several times he wanted to run to the rail tracks and put his head on the track to get killed by the train. Often two to three adults were needed to control him.

When we locked him inside the house he would hang a cot by two of its legs on the top of the courtyard wall, climb the cot, and jump outside. He would then run towards the rail tracks. Often he became an uncontrollable beast who would shove everyone aside. Such incidents were the most difficult ones in our childhood. All the kids used to pray to god that nothing happened that night. In arguments with Baoji, Amma would never take a back seat even if she got physically thrashed by him. Those were the dreadful years of our lives. Neighbours, co-workers, and visitors to the area, in fact the whole railway staff got to know Baoji's shameless behaviour. We were made fun of by others. Remarks would be made: "there goes that *Sharabi's* (drunk man's) son." We just hung our heads in shame. This was a very gruesome, difficult, and cursed childhood. But come next morning, Baoji would be a different man. If he remembered what he had done the night before, he would avoid eye contact with all. That was his way of apologizing. And, when he sat down to do his daily *pooja*, he seemed to be the most polite, gentle, and calm individual. Often I found it so hard to try and reconcile these diametrically opposed dimensions of Baoji's personality. After Rajeev had left for Delhi, I had to assume more responsibilities in Hapur.

Despite all his misdemeanours and idiosyncrasies, I still loved my father. I couldn't afford not to. I was deeply attached to him emotionally. Basically, he was a kind and compassionate man. He was also a highly emotional human being. I remember many acts of his kindness. One day the family was going to visit Bawal, our ancestral town. We had to change the train in Delhi. It was still the time of meter gage BB&CI (Bombay Baroda and Central Indian) Railway connecting Delhi to Rewari, Alwar, Jaipur, Ajmer, and beyond. Baoji had a very close boyhood personal friend, Parmanand, who worked at Sarai Rohalla railway station Baoji got off the train at Sarai Rohalla railway platform and went to look for Parmanand to say hello. But a tragedy had occurred a couple of days earlier. While on duty, Parmanand was attaching two bogies in the shunting area of the railway yard. Suddenly the train from behind moved by mistake of the driver. Parmanand was crushed to death. Baoji had no knowledge of that. He decided that all of us would get off the train at Sarai Rohalla. We went to Permanand's railway quarter to console his widow and family. He was weeping loudly, hugging Parmanand's children. I had never seen this personality dimension of Baoji prior to this. We took the next train to Bawal.

We were always treated well in Bawal. My aunt, Kaushalya, lived there with her husband, her children, Radhey, Dhanni, Shiela, and Urmila. They all lived with *Babaji* in Bawal. Babaji had long retired as stationmaster of Bawal. Dadi had passed away long before I was born. Babaji' cousin's widow, named Badamo, lived with him. Kaushalya Bhua's husband, named Nandlal, was a priest by profession. He was a *ghar jamai* (one who lives with in-laws). To be a *ghar jamai* was, and still is, considered a shameful option necessitated by economic exigency. Nandlal Phuphaji was often insulted by Babaji. He would say: *"Saala karta to kuchch hai nahi, ghar baithe baithe bachche paida karta rehta hai aur saural ki kamai khata hai"* ("Good for nothing fellow, does nothing, keeps producing kids and lives off his in-laws".).

Many years later, Nandlal took the insult seriously, and left Babaji's home in Bawal, never to come back and nowhere to be found. He was searched all over India, at religious centres and pilgrimage places. There was no trace of him. He left Bhua with one more child, a boy named Mahesh. Against all odds, Bhua believed that her husband was still alive and she lived like a *suhagan* (married woman), wearing bangles in her hands and putting *sindoor* at the parting of her hair, both being signs of matrimony. But after Shiela's and Radhey's marriages, she began to believe that her husband was no more and she started living like a widow. Dhanni, the same age as

Rajeev, worked in a textile mill in Bombay. He died young. Radhey found a job in the Municipal Corporation of Delhi, and he took Bhua and the rest of the family with him to his house in Delhi. But that was much later, in the 1960s. Radhey had lived with Amar for about a year in Delhi before he was successful in finding a job.

Being from Bawal, Baoji had a lot of friends and extensive social network in the small town. He enjoyed a lot of respect in Bawal. He also had many drinking buddies there. We used to have several reunions in Bawal. The whole extended family would gather. Amma, Badamo Dadi, Chachi, and Bhua would be in the kitchen cooking. The boys would be fooling around, jumping in the village *Johad* (pond), and swimming, eating *pakodas, samosas,* and the famous Bawal *barfi.* Occasionally, they would take the train to Rewari, the next train station, to see a cinema. Bawal had no cinema halls. Going to Bawal was a time for merriment and fun.

I felt the same way visiting my *Nani* (mother's mother) in Milakpur. My Nani was old. She had become a widow rather early and she had lost her husband and two sons to tuberculosis. To go to Milakpur from Gajraula, Umartali, or Hapur, we had to change the train in Rewari. We had to get off at Narnaul railway station. There were no roads then to Milakpur. The only mode of transportation was camel. So, we had to travel on a camel's back from Narnaul to Milakpur, a distance of more than 15 kms. Our backs would be sour, we would be hungry, and we would be served leftover food by our Mamiji: chapatis, a raw onion, *gur,* and sweet mango pickle. The ordinary menu tasted so great. We were just so hungry. The town of

Behror was just a few kms away. Nandlal Phuphaji's hometown was Behror. Shiela's wedding was performed in Behror. I have a distinct memory of that wedding. Kaushalya Bhua's children were all fair-skinned. Radhey was older than Hari but younger than Amar. Urmila and Karuna were the same age.

As a 16 year old Rajeev had a tendency to flirt with girls where we lived in the railway colony. There was a pretty teenage girl, named Padma, who had a crush on Rajeev. They found every excuse to see each other. Letters were exchanged between them. Padma lived in a nearby quarter. She used to embroider Rajeev's name on handkerchiefs and give them to Rajeev as gifts. This was a "puppy love" of the teenagers and ended when Rajeev moved to Delhi for his architecture program.

In the railway quarter in Hapur, Amma had a very peculiar problem. A monkey who lived on trees near our quarter took a liking for Amma's clothes. Whenever Amma took a bath and left fresh clothes on a cot, the monkey would come down and run away with her blouse or petticoat. Amma would call me loudly to help get her clothes back from the monkey. I would first ask the monkey to return the clothes. When that didn't work I would threaten the monkey with a *laathi*. That too did not work most of the time. Then I would have to give the monkey a leftover *roti* to distract his attention. He would let go of the clothe(s) and go for the *roti*. Eventually we had to get rid of the monkey by burning fire under the trees.

Back to Hapur again, everyone was doing whatever they could to help prepare for Binno's wedding. In the summer of 1954, after Rajeev had left for Delhi, Baoji brought the son of our traditional *Nai* (barber) from Bawal.

His name was Ram Kumar and everyone called him 'Ram Kumar Nai ka' so as not to confuse him with Ram Kumar Chachaji. Ram Kumar Nai ka did many household chores and helped Amma in many ways. Baoji was able to get him a license to become a coolie at the Hapur railway station.

The *baraat* for Binno's wedding was to stay for three days. Over 200 *baraatis* were expected. A large *dharamshala* was booked for the marriage party. Halwaai (sweet maker) and cooks had been hired. Baoji made arrangements for overflow of family and friends to stay with friends and colleagues in the railway staff. Despite his "reputation", he still had a lot of good will among people. Arrangement was made for a mare to be ridden by the groom for *ghurcharhi,* and a band was hired. On the morning of December 3, 1954, the baraat arrived at Hapur railway station. All the elder family members were at the railway platform to welcome and greet the party. Mool Chand *Mausaji* fired a rifle shot in the air to ceremoniously announce the arrival of the *baraat*. Rajeev had arranged for three cars to bring the groom, his father, *Taoji* (father's older brother), two brothers, and three brothers-in-law to the dharamshala. All of this needed planning and precision and Rajeev and his friends proved true to the task.

There were a number of ceremonies prior to the marriage proper. It was young boys' duty to serve food to the baraat members three times a day. The marriage ceremony proper was scheduled for the early morning hours of December 5. Karuna and I decided to leave the house around 8:30 pm after supper, and took a rickshaw to Shankar talkies and went to see the movie

Biraj Bahu. We just wanted to pass time before *phere* or *saptapadi* (seven rounds around the fire undertaken by the bride and groom).

The marriage was over. After the *bidaai* ceremony on December 5, the marriage party left in the evening. I accompanied Binno to Rampur Katra along with the marriage party. After four days of stay and many more rituals there, I brought Binno back to Hapur. Since she was older than me, I did not address her with her first name; instead I called her *jeejee*. The generic term for brother in Hindi is *bhai*. But I had three older brothers, so I had to use qualifiers with the generic kinship term to distinguish one from the others. I called Amar by the term *Bhai Sahib*; Hari was called simply *Bhai*; and Rajeev was addressed as Chhote Bhai. Hindi kinship terminology is highly descriptive. Terms for address are far more descriptive as opposed to terms of reference where some lumping of kinship comes into play.

After Binno's marriage, things calmed down quite a bit. And a new routine was established. Having invested so much time in the wedding, it was now time for me to concentrate on my studies. The U.P. Board examinations were held in April. In the examination students were assigned a roll number. My roll number was 12788. I thought I had done well in the final exams. The U.P. Board exam results were published in a special issue of the newspaper. One newspaper printed the results with students names. My name was missing from the result column of my college. Even though I was confident, I became crestfallen. Amma started making noises: "Didn't I say he spends so much time playing games? Now he has failed!" Baoji just didn't believe that I could fail. Two hours later, a train brought a huge bundle of Amrit Bazar Patrika, a newspaper from Allahabad. It published results by the roll numbers. My roll number featured among those getting first division. I also got a distinction in mathematics. Baoji hugged me tightly and I saw tears of happiness in his eyes. Now it was his turn to get back at Amma.

7

SIMBHAOLI

Soon after my high school graduation, Baoji received orders of transfer as permanent station master at the railway station named Simbhaoli. Initially both Baoji and I were unhappy as I had become used to Hapur. But transfer orders cannot be challenged. Baoji had to move to Simbhaoli. His friends and colleagues advised him to put me in a hostel and attend Intermediate College in Hapur. Raghubir Singh Kisan Intermediate College in Simbhaoli was located in a predominantly rural area. No one from that college had ever received first division in F.Sc. My father was adamant. He did not want to put me in a hostel. His retort was: "it does not matter where my son goes to college. If he is smart he will pass with first division." I was surprised at his confidence in me. Time to buckle up, I said to myself. I had to prove Baoji was right.

Simbhaoli was not too far from Hapur, just three train stations east of Hapur on Delhi-Moradabad line. It was a sugar mill town. There were two assistant station masters under Baoji who worked the night shifts while Baoji did the day (8 am to 4 pm) shift. R.S.K. Intermediate College was close to the train station, located just 300 meters across from the rail tracks. Alongside the college there was the boys' hostel. Most of the students were from the outlying villages; only a few came from the town. It was a co-ed college but there were only a handful of female students. The college also had a middle and high school component. Karuna joined this school in grade 7. There were a much larger number of girls in the school than in the college. The landowners in villages surrounding Simbhaoli grew sugar cane and once harvested, sugar cane was brought to the sugar mill in Simbhaoli. There was a large mill complex, the factory itself, and the residences of the owners and mill workers. The complex was tightly supervised and there were watchmen, dogs, and other security staff. The market in Simbhaoli was a little less than a kilometer away from the train station by the main road that led to Garhmukteshwar to the east and Hapur and beyond to the west.

During the early winter months when sugar cane was harvested, the roads leading to Simbhaoli, the streets of the town, and the Simbhaoli marketplace were littered with sugar cane peels that became slippery if it rained. It was usually the porter or me, or we both together, who went to the market to buy vegetables, soap, fruits, grocery items, stationery, etc. The books for the classes were only available in Hapur. Both Karuna and I made a trip to Hapur to buy the books. There were very convenient passenger train connections between Simbhaoli and Hapur. The train left Simbhaoli at 2:15 pm and reached Hapur at 2:45 pm. One could take a rickshaw to the cinema hall or to the market, see the matinee show, or do the shopping, take the rickshaw back to the train station in Hapur, catch the 6:45 pm train and be home in Simbhaoli by 7:15 pm. Karuna and I did this numerous times, especially to go see a movie in Hapur.

Baoji bought a cow in Simbhaoli. She was a beautiful creature, mostly white in colour with very light brown spots on her body. Baoji named her Gomti, and lovingly called her Goma. He became very attached to her. Many times in his drunken condition I saw Baoji hug her and speak to her. In a few months, Gomti delivered a young one, a female, and she became a source of milk. We all loved cow milk. Both Baoji and Amma knew how to milk the cow. I also learned to do the same from Baoji. Cow fodder had to be bought and Gomti was also sent to graze, along with a group of other cattle, during the day with a cowherd, at some distance from the railway station.

The students at the college were rustic, not polite, and difficult to make friends with. A large number stayed at the hostel. But likely twice as many commuted daily, on foot, on bicycle, or by bus. There was no one of college going age on the railway staff. So Karuna and I were a bit unique in this regard. I missed playing cricket that I had become so used to at the school in Hapur. I discussed the matter with the principal of R. S. K. Intermediate College in Simbhaoli, suggesting to him that the college should have a cricket team. Surprisingly I found enthusiastic support to the idea from the principal and he was willing to have me take the leadership in this. Only field hockey, soccer, and volleyball were played at the college until then. The idea of building a cricket pitch was opposed. So we settled on a matting wicket. I was given enough cash by the college to buy the equipment from Hapur. I ordered 15 willow bats, a jute matting wicket, four dozen cherry colour balls, two sets of wicketkeeper pads and gloves, a dozen set of batting pads, two sets of six wickets, four sets of bails, and fifteen caps and sweaters. The players were to buy their own shoes, white pairs of pants, and shirts.

Cricket equipment was delivered to the college in Simbhaoli in a week after I had ordered it. Now we needed a team. The principal sent a circular to the college students to sign up for their interest in cricket. Surprisingly, about 100 people signed up. Many of them had not played cricket ever. Some had very limited experience while about half a dozen had played elsewhere. We had practice almost everyday for one hour under the supervision of a cricket "coach" from Hapur. I was chosen the captain of the team and we finally settled on a 15-member team. The cricket team had to share the same field with the soccer team and the field hockey team. On a practice basis, the three sports had only one hour each on the field from Monday to Saturday, and two hours each on Sundays. At that time Saturday was a working day in India, rather than a part of the weekend.

Starting in late September of 1955, our cricket team started playing matches with teams from other colleges. Most matches were played on Sundays. Baoji did not know anything about cricket, but with his son being the captain of the team, he started to take interest and even came to watch a match or two for an hour or two. He was quite proud of me since I was the only member of the family who became the captain of a sports team. Baoji's drinking continued unabated. His arguments with Amma again picked up steam. Binno was now spending most of her time in her *sasural* with her in-laws. I visited Rampur Katra twice during our two-year stay in Simbhaoli. One night after drinking some alcohol, Baoji got in a strange mood. He lectured me about the benefits of a good education, and that my first priority should be success in academics and sports should be secondary. He also regretted the fact of all four sons he had none that chose a railway career. He urged and pleaded with me that during the second year of my F.Sc., I must appear for the railway public service commission examination. I agreed to that. Baoji was elated. After all, this Bawal family of Sharma's had a history of serving in the railways.

In the quarter adjoining ours lived Sanjeev Gulati, one of the two assistant station masters. He was young and good looking and had a very pretty Punjabi wife. Whenever she saw me going to or returning from the college, she would give me this amazing smile. For an adolescent boy this made his day. She could not have been older than 22 or 23. One day, I saw a kite come flying towards our quarter and getting lodged on its roof. I immediately took a cot, hung it by two legs on the courtyard wall and climbed on the wall to get to the roof. As soon as I reached the top of the wall, I saw Gulati's beautiful wife taking a bath. She was totally naked with sprawling light brown hair and very round shaped breasts that had tiny darkish brown nipples. I could not take my eyes off her. She suddenly sensed someone watching her. She turned around, stood up, and I could see her completely naked, pubic hair and all. She had this strange expression on her face, an embarrassing smile, some anger and complaint. She ran away from the courtyard. I went up on the roof, picked up the kite, came down and removed the cot from the wall. I do not believe anyone else knew about this unexpected feast for my eyes.

Initially Gulati and Baoji got along well, but tension began to develop within the two when Baoji had been in Simbhaoli for about six months. Part of the reason for the worsening of their relationship had to do with the field of maize that Baoji planted right next to the quarters. Gulati thought that it took away from the view from the quarters. Being his senior, Baoji did not give any credibility to Gulati's objections. They also had a disagreement about the share they got from *ooper ki amdani* (bribe money) generated by selling passes to milkmen and other businessmen who used trains to transport their commodities, such as mangoes (in season) and *khoaa* (a byproduct of milk made by boiling milk used by sweet makers in the larger centres). In 1955, Baoji was 50 years old whereas Gulati was almost half his age, very fit, trim and agile. If there were to be a physical fight between the two, Baoji would have no chance at all. The other assistant stationmaster, Ram Gupta, was sometimes on Baoji's side and at other times leaned toward Gulati.

We learned that Gulati's wife was pregnant. She began to show in her third month. One winter morning when Gomti was being taken for grazing, she came across Gulati's wife. I found out her name was Preeti. She was wearing a dark red *shalwar kameez* suit and *dupatta*. Some trigger went to Gomti's head and she ran at Preeti in an agitated state. I was studying outside. I jumped up and ran, shouted to Goma and Preeti and jumped between them. Now Goma was mad at me. I suddenly mustered up a lot of strength, and grabbed both her horns. The cow was now fighting me. With both her force and my resistance, one of her horns broke off. She yelled in pain and started to shake her head vigorously. Amma brought some water. It took three people to detach the horn completely. Gomti was in terrible pain. Amma applied a paste of *haldi* (turmeric) and *chuna* (lime water). After a few minutes Goma calmed down. She did not go to graze that day. It took her almost a whole month to recover. Preeti was so ever thankful to me. I had saved both her and the foetus. I was very proud of my courage and agility. Gulati thanked me profusely. Baoji was upset that Goma lost her horn but highly praised me.

One afternoon I was playing field hockey on the college grounds and a tall Jat student hit a hard shot that I could not avoid and the hard white ball hit me on my left chest. I fell down and blacked out for a few minutes. Everyone, I was told later, panicked and one of the players ran to the train station to inform Baoji who came running to the field. Water was thrown on my face and I came to. Baoji took me home. Another day, again when I was practicing cricket on the college grounds, the porter came running and said that Gulati and Baoji had gotten into a physical fight and that Gulati had pushed Baoji into the maize field and Baoji fell down. This time it was my turn to bail Baoji out. I helped him up. He wasn't hurt physically but his ego took a beating. I took the evening train to Hapur and told Rajeev's and my friends what had happened. Having stayed overnight in Hapur, I came back to Simhaoli next morning accompanied by five young men. When we reached Simbhaoli station, Gulati was approaching the end of his shift. These young men went straight to the station and grabbed Gulati's shirt collar and punched him twice. Gulati was warned by the young men that if he were to do anything stupid to Baoji again, he would be thrashed. The poor fellow, getting outnumbered, felt very scared and walked like a frightened cat to his quarter, as Baoji came to his day shift, walking as a lion and with a wide grin on his face.

That night, after alcohol went into his system, Baoji yelled some choice words at Gulati. This would cause further friction between them and, as it turned out later, Baoji had a very heavy price to pay for this. I had a crush at a girl named Geeta Rao. She was the daughter of the railway overseer. She was my age, with a dark complexion, and had long black hair, and beautiful eyes. Her brother was in the college and I knew him well. Geeta and I started spending some time together. There was a wide canal before the eastern outer signal of Simbhaoli. The canal on its eastern side was lined with *jamun* trees. The trees of this berry like fruit were large and the fruit was at least ten feet high above the ground. The fruit ripened in the rainy season just like mangoes. I would climb up the tree, take hold of a branch and shake it hard. The *jamuns* will fall to the ground and Geeta would pick them up. We would then pick a spot to sit down and eat them. The fruit had a pit that we had to spit out. Our tongues and lips would turn purple after eating the juicy and sweet fruit. On some of these outings Karuna would join us. Although she liked Geeta, she was more interested in jamun. Also in the rainy season, a vendor would be selling corn on the cob, roasting the cob on the slow burning cow dung fire. After the cob was roasted, the vendor would apply lime juice, salt and *chat masala* on it. It was one of those rare seasonal treats.

My courtship with Geeta lasted for over a year. I was invited by her to her house for tea and met her parents who were quite friendly to me. I remember Geeta using vast amount of talcum powder on her neck, upper arms, even face. She carried that fragrant smell wherever she went. Our family used Life Buoy bath soap and Sunlight for washing clothes. A *dhobi* (washerman) used to come every 10 days or so to take the dirty laundry for washing and ironing. I used to prepare the list of clothes going out with the *dhobi* and match that list with the ready laundry when the *dhobi* came. The cycle would be repeated again and again. Under wears and undershirts were hand washed at home. Amma and Karuna used the latrine at home whereas Baoji and I went out in the open fields to relieve ourselves. We carried a *lota* (small metal water pitcher) full of water to wash afterwards. Baoji was a very clean person. He paid a lot of attention to his teeth and rinsing his mouth after eating. He never in his life used tooth brush and tooth paste, but a *datun (a* short tender stick of *Neem* or *Keekar* tree). All his sons and daughters, and Amma did the same. We will chew the datum on one end, work it into a soft brush and then use this brush briskly on our teeth before rinsing our mouths. These *datuns* had an amazing natural cleaning quality. Baoji never had any issues with his teeth; not even a single cavity. Amma's was another story. She loved sweets and did not take good care of her teeth. All of her teeth were pulled out before she was 40 years old and she started to wear dentures that were fitted and bought in Delhi.

Amar moved from Karol Bagh to Rohtak Road in late 1955, to a two-bedroom accommodation. On January 1, 1956, the whole family with the exception of Binno gathered in Simbhaoli. It was my 14th birthday. We had a fun time as Amma made some really festive food: *poori, aloo* (potatoes), *kashiphal* (yellow squash), *bhindi* (okra), kheer (rice pudding), and *gajar* (carrot) *halwa.* It was the kind of food made only on festive occasions. Amar had a German Rolyflex camera that he had bought. He took several photographs that are cherished to this day. There was a film unit from Bombay shooting for a film at the premises of the sugar mill. The actors were Karan Diwan and Geeta Bali. Baoji invited them inside his office at the train station and served them tea, biscuits, and pastry. Karan Diwan was a good looking and sociable individual. For a very well-known and extrovert actor, Geeta Bali kept rather quiet.

One late morning I was studying outside. It was early winter time. I went inside the house for a glass of water. I saw Amma sitting on an *aasan* (a small piece of woolen rug), moving the beads of her *mala* (a sort of a necklace consisting of wooden beads) with her fingers and reciting some *pooja* words slowly. Although she was wearing glasses, her eyes were closed and her head covered with her sari. She also had a shawl covering the upper part of her body. Simbhaoli was notorious for a very large number of domestic flies. If you quickly swung your hand with an open fist in one direction and suddenly closed the fist, you would have caught a handful of flies. I was an expert at doing this. Very rarely would I miss catching a fly. The presence of a sugar mill brought down huge amounts of black, sugar-laden soot to the ground. Naturally the flies would flock to this sweet dust. As I walked towards the pitcher full of water, I saw the flies lifting above the ground in front of Amma in a sort of wave. I was in horrified shock to see a snake crawling on the ground only inches in front of Amma. I yelled: "Amma, *sanp*". ("Amma, a snake"). Amma opened her eyes, and seeing a snake in front of her she was terrified and fell backwards.

The snake didn't bite Amma, but it was also frightened due to the noise. It crawled towards the *chakki* (flour mill) that Amma used daily to grind fresh flour from wheat grains. There was a mouse hole in the ground at the corner of the wall where the chakki was situated. Amma said: "Take the snake out, otherwise it will bite me." I called the porter and by using a hammer and chisel he opened up and widened the whole. All this time I was standing beside him armed with a *lathi* (thick and large wooden staff). Finally the porter found the snake and took it out with the lathi. The snake seemed half dead, as it had eaten a mouse, or two, but could not swallow and choked. We dragged the snake out of the house. It was well over a meter long. We killed the snake to end its misery. With the blow of *lathi* on its neck, out popped the mouse still not fully dead. We decided to cremate the dead snake near the garden.

In early 1956 Bhabhi got pregnant. Baoji was so happy. Bhabhi had two miscarriages before. Amma used to advise her on how to sustain pregnancy. A month before the childbirth, Amma went to Delhi to take care of Bhabhi, and do cooking, etc. Baoji, Karuna and I were in Simbhaoli without Amma for the first time. Our food came from a restaurant in the market. It rained heavily during the summer of 1956 in north India. As a result, the River

Yamuna crossed the danger mark due to flooding. We got a telegram in Simbhaoli that Bhabhi gave birth to a healthy seven-pound baby. We were all thrilled, most of all Baoji who became a *dada* (paternal grandfather) for the first time. His happiness knew no bounds. *Laddoos* were bought and distributed to the entire railway staff. But we had to wait for a week before we could travel to Delhi to see the newborn He was named Subhash, with a nickname Babboo. Subhash was born on October 2, 1956. He shared his birthday with Mahatma Gandhi.

Like all grandfathers, Baoji was tearfully happy and emotional. He hugged Amar and he blessed Bhabhi. All brothers were there in the small flat on Rohtak Road. There was a new cinema hall just within a block on the other side of the street. The cinema hall was named Liberty and we all went to see the film Tajmahal that was running. It starred Pradeep Kumar and Bina Roy. Amma, Bhabhi, and the newborn stayed home. In a few days, Amma, Baoji, Karuna and I returned to Simbhaoli. Amar was now planning to rent a three room flat in an almost new area close to the Delhi University campus. The address, 2/28 Roop Nagar, Delhi-6, would be the new abode of the Sharma's for many years.

Hari had struggled in Ajmer initially and then in Alwar. He had found a job as a lower division clerk in the customs division of foreign post in Alwar. On Amar's insistence, he was able to manage a transfer to New Delhi at the Mathura Road office. His move to Delhi occurred in the middle of 1955 when Amar, his wife, and Rajeev were still in Karol Bagh. Hari was a calmer person, somewhat of an introvert at that time, very handsome with beautiful and expressive eyes like that of his favourite film actor Guru Dutt. He had tried to get his B.A. degree earlier through a college in Ajmer at the University of Rajasthan but failed. Then, he attempted again, this time privately, through Agra University. He passed that time, but barely with a low third division marks. At that point in his life, academic achievement was not his forte. Baoji worried about him a lot. He was not too happy that his three oldest sons were out of his control and that Amar had assumed more of the patriarchal authority. This bothered him a lot and the resentment often spilled out when he was drunk.

Back in Simbhaoli it was a tough studying time for Karuna and me. We slept on different cots in the same room that was connected by a door to the other bedroom where Amma slept. This door was left open. Amma used to wake me up at 4 am. When I did not respond to his call to get up, she would use a large stick from her room to hit me, gently at first but harder if I failed to respond. There was no electricity in the railway quarters and the train stations. We had to use lanterns, fuelled by kerosene oil, in order to study. Often I would dose off and sleep, with my head resting on top of the lantern. That would burn my hair and leave an acrid smell around my forehead and face for some time. Karuna did not get up at 4 am. It was my responsibility to wake her up at 5:30 am. Naturally, I used to boss her around. But I also loved her immensely. We made a good team for watching movies. She was always the one who I pushed to go to Baoji at the railway station. He would look at her and ask with a smile: "*Cinema jana hai*" ("Want to go to see a film"?). He would always give her three to five rupees that covered the cost of movie tickets for two, rickshaw both ways from Hapur railway station to the cinema hall, and some snacks. We did not need to buy train tickets. As children of a railway employee, we had a free train pass in a second class compartment that had leather seats. Third class compartments had wooden seats. Karuna and I enjoyed the luxury of traveling in second class.

One day we were planning on a movie outing to Hapur. But there were a lot of people at the train station in Baoji's office. Baoji seemed very stressed. As Karuna entered the station office, Baoji looked at her angrily and with a movement of his head, signaled "no" and waved at her to go home. We got worried. What was going on? While Karuna went to the quarter, I stuck around at the railway platform. Upon asking, the junior staff informed me that the people in Baoji's office were from the anti-corruption branch of the Northern Railway and had come to Simbhaoli unannounced by a car to surprise Baoji. I immediately knew that Gulati had something to do with this. May be he needed another thrashing. But this was serious stuff. Although everyone in the railway system had *ooper ki amdani*, it was still illegal. Baoji had sold some passes to the milkmen before he started seliing train tickets. More than likely, as I learned later, a total of thirty rupees as illegal money. He had to get rid of that before the anti-corruption men were to start counting the total cash in Baoji's possession. Even though he had two guys watch him, one on the left and the other on the right, he was able to slip out all thirty rupees to the passengers as he gave them more than the owed change after the purchase of the ticket. Baoji knew many of the passengers as they were frequent travelers. He must have made some gesture, may be the wink of an eye or whatever, so that they wouldn't express any surprise or say something.

Baoji did that very well. Apparently, when the counting of the cash began, there wasn't even a single paisa extra in his possession. But a cloud of suspension remained. Baoji felt that his integrity had been compromised and that in the eye of his station staff he became a fallible human being. His ego was bruised and suddenly he seemed vulnerable. His drinking increased in quantity. Soon after this incident, Geeta and his brother came to visit our house for the first time. Amma took great pride in keeping the quarter clean. The house was white washed ever year before Diwali. The pictures of various Hindu gods and goddesses were framed in glass and hanged neatly on the walls. Being from Andhra Pradesh, I thought that Geeta's family would not be familiar with the pantheon of Hindu gods and goddesses. So I decided to point out to them: "This is Ram"; "this is Krishna and Radha"; "this is Shiva"; "this is Ganesha". The picture of Hanuman was a bit high. I don't know what came in my head; I picked up a sandal and threw it gently at the picture and said to the visitors, "and, this is Hanuman." Baoji had entered the room when I threw the sandal. He was red with anger. Right in front of Geeta and her brother, he slapped me hard. I realized my mistake right away and with folded hands apologized to Baoji. That was the end of the visit. That night, after a drink or two, Baoji came in the room, stood in front of Hanumanji's photo with folded hands. Hanuman was his ishta devata (personal god). He said: "*Woh bachcha hai, nadan hai; use samajh nahin hai. Use maaf kar dijiye Hanumanji"* ("He is a kid; he is innocent; he does not understand. Please pardon him Hanumanji".)

My cricket team did not do too well initially. We lost matches to Hapur and Bijnor. I told my team members that we had to practice harder to win. We needed to ball better, bat better, field better, and play better as a team, in unison. Then some thing dramatic happened. There was a professional team in Amroha consisting of senior players who had been playing for years. They wanted to boost up our morale and wanted to play a friendly match against us. We took it as a challenge. We had nothing to lose. We played a solid game. I excelled in that match, scoring 78 runs with several fours. Our team scored 154 runs, way beyond our expectations. It was a Sunday. Baoji also came to watch the match and clapped whenever I scored a boundary. I had hit seven fours against a very good team. Now came the Amroha team to bat. They had a solid opening stand of 38 runs. Imtiaz Ahmad was their opening batsman and captain. I came to ball medium pacers, and in my very first over, I clean bowled Imtiaz Ahmad. Then there was a succession of Amroha batsmen who got out cheaply. I had the match bowling figure of 6 for 37. Amroha team was all out for 123. We had the most convincing win by 32 runs. The spectators cheered and danced. Baoji remarked: *"Mehnat ka phal sadev meetha hota hai"* (Hard labour always pays off.) I saw Baoji so happy after a long time. Following the win over Amroha, we won three straight matches, two at home against Bijnor and Khurja. Then we beat Hapur in an away game. That was the end of the season for playing cricket as the final examinations were only a month away.

It was late February, 1957. It was a Tuesday. Baoji had a fasting day; he did not drink. I was studying at the table. Baoji came close to the photograph of Hanumanji and said slowly, but I heard it: "Balawali; why Balawali? What is my fault?" His muttering made sense to me immediately. Baoji had received orders for a transfer to Balawali, a much smaller railway station near Najibabad, close to Dehradun. There were no schools in Balawali. The nearest town with a school was Najibabad. While it would help Karuna, there was nothing for me there.

I wrote my F.Sc. board examinations in April of 1957. The result came out in May. I passed with first division standing, and distinctions in mathematics and chemistry. Two other students from R.S.K. Intermediate College also received first division, a first for the college. I topped the class at the college. But I was also concerned about my future. On Baoji's insistence I had also appeared for the Railway Public Service Commission examination and passed in a high percentile. But I was not keen to join the railway service. This must have disappointed Baoji.

8

BALAWALI

Balawali was a neat little place, fair bit cooler in climate compared to Hapur and Simbhaoli. It was quite close to Dehradun, and Haridwar and Rishikesh were only a bit more than two hours away by train. Balawali had a glass factory where they made glasses, juice sets, jugs, and other glass objects. The railway quarter in Balawali was similar to that elsewhere. During the transfer, one compartment on the freight train was for Gomti and the other for household possessions. Amma had become an expert in moving for so many transfers. Within a few months of our arrival in Balawali, the news came that Binno had given birth to a healthy baby girl who was named Shashikala. Baoji had now become a *Nana* too in addition to being a *Dada*. In the month of May I was sent to Rampur Katra to bring Binno and the newborn to Balawali. To reach Rampur Katra was arduous as a river had to be crossed to reach the village. During the rainy season, the river would overflow with water. One had to fold the pants up to and above the knees, and carry the baggage on the head and shoes/sandals in the hands well above the water. I had encountered such a scenario several times during my visits to Rampur Katra. Luckily, we were spared that ordeal this time.

It was a happy time with Binno and the baby. Together with her and the baby we made trips to Dehradun, and to Haridwar and Rishikesh. In Rishikesh, I remember walking on the suspension bridge called Lakshman Jhoola. Ganga River was so clean and swift in Rishikesh and Haridwar. We also visited the glass factory in Balawali and Baoji bought a glass set for juice or *Shikanji* (lime juice shake with added sugar and ice) for Binno and one set for the family use in Balawali. My stay in Balawali was limited. I helped to admit Karuna in a school in Najibabad. She was in grade 9 now. She was a better than average student, not very good in mathematics, okay in Hindi and English, good in history and general knowledge but hopeless in science subjects. Arrangements were made for her to stay with the family of one of Baoji's railway friends in Najibabad who was paid a nominal amount for Karuna's room and board. But as things turned out later, Karuna did not like the school in Najibabad, and dropped out of school and stayed home for a year.

I guess my academic fate was pre-decided. I went the route of my two older brothers and moved to Delhi to live with Amar, Bhabhi, Hari, Rajeev, and Babboo. It was crowded even in a three-room flat. I moved to 2/28 Roop Nagar in the month of June in 1957.

9

DELHI

Coming to Delhi was both exciting and frightening for me. I was only 15 years old. I had never lived in a large city. Although in 1957 Delhi had a population of just around 4 million, it was huge, bigger than anything I could have imagined. Roop Nagar was a clean new area, right next to the famous GT (Grand Trunk) Road. To the south was the well-known Ghantaghar with its big clock and Sabzi Mandi. To the west was Shakti Nagar. The GT Road ran parallel to the *Ganda Nallah* (sewage drain) that overflowed in the rainy season, and north of Shakti Nagar was Rana Pratap Bagh; beyond that Model Town, Kingsway Camp, and Indira Nagar. Opposite to Roop Nagar on the east of GT Road was Kamla Nagar with a large market. Bungalow Road defined the parameter of Kamla Nagar and beyond it in the east lay the main campus of the University of Delhi. There were several colleges on this campus: Ramjas College, Kirorimal College, Hindu College, Ramjas College, St. Stephens College, Hansraj College, Shriram College of Commerce, and Miranda House (the elite college for women with its famous hostel). Maurice Nagar was the main bus stop for all students. It was walking distance from our flat in Roop Nagar, no more than a ten minutes' walk.

It was my desire to do a B.Sc. degree in Physics, Chemistry, and Mathematics to be followed by a Master's degree in Chemistry, my favourite subject. I applied to St. Stephens College, arguably the top men's college at Delhi University. I was admitted to the college. I was so happy and so were all members of the family including Baoji. I attended classes for a week, and was gradually buying books. But then came a rude shock. While in a class, I was summoned by the principal of St. Stephens College to his office. I had never met him. What he told me was a real downer.

"You can't attend this college or, for that matter, any college at the University of Delhi". Not knowing what he meant, I looked at him with puzzlement.

"But what have I done, sir?"

"Nothing at all. In fact, you are a brilliant student. But you are two years too young."

"Is it a crime to be too young and very good at studies?, I asked.

"No, but the university has a policy about age. A student has to be physically mature to be accepted at the university level. This is not something against you personally. It applies to everybody. I am sorry."

I had to leave St. Stephens College. After talking this over with all in the family, it was decided that I will do B.Sc. in Ghaziabad, a nearby town in Uttar Pradesh. Mahanand Mission Harijan (M.M.H.) College in Ghaziabad was affiliated to Agra University that had no age restriction for its students. Thus started a new routine for me. It was hard, time consuming and tough on the body. But I had no other choice. I was easily accepted at M.M.H. College. Baoji bought a new cycle for me. I had to get up early in the morning, around 4:30 am, do my bodily things, take a shower, get dressed, have breakfast which Bhabhi made, and bike to the Delhi train station. I would park my bike at the bike stand near the train station, take the 6:40 am Sealdah Express, get off at the Ghaziabad train station, a 35-minute train ride, and then walk to the college, little less than a km from the train station. Bhabhi would give my lunch, 4 *paranthas* (bread shallow fried in ghee or oil on a flat pan) and dry vegetable curry that she would have cooked in the morning before anyone else even got up. I would have eaten two paranthas for my breakfast. At the end of classes, I would do everything in reverse, and come home by about 4:00 or 4:30 pm. Rain or shine, this was my routine for six days a week.

It was not the best routine, but there was no other option for me. I studied on the train, after coming home in the late afternoon, and at night. Sundays used to be hectic as well. Everyone did their laundry, taking turns in the bathroom, or at the outside tap in the large courtyard that was shared by all tenants in the building. Our landlord lived on the first floor; we did on the ground floor. There was a tenant living in the mazanine, that was barely 8 feet by 8 feet with a low (about five and a half feet high) ceiling. We had our own bathroom for bathing, and there were two latrines that were shared by us and the dweller in the mazanine. Sometimes members of our landlord's family would also use the latrine. The front gate of the building was exclusively for our use, while everyone else used the side door that opened to the lane that ran perpendicular to the street on which the main gate was located. Space was tight, and in our flat there were four brothers and the wife of the eldest one. Occasionally, Baoji and Amma or other relatives would visit us in the flat. Then it became really tight. In winter months there were three beds in the corner room where Hari, Rajeev and I slept. The living room was also Amar and Bhabhi's bedroom. The middle bedroom had a cot, a Godrej almirah, and several boxes and suitcases stored in it. All the bedding was also stored in that room during the day.

All four brothers were at the dinning table for the dinner which we ate around 9 pm. I had a huge appetite then. So, I would have helped myself with two samosas and chickpeas at a shop on the main intersection nearby on G.T. Road. Bhabhi was the lone cook. She also cleaned after meals. She was a hardworking soul who did everything without complaint. Amar worked late at night in the living room/bedroom. Bhabhi would just have to sleep with her head turned away from the tube light with Babboo lying next to her. Being an artist, Amar would paint or work on some project such as creating a mural for the exhibition grounds, or illustrating a book. This would fetch him extra income. Amar controlled the budget of this extended family. Probably "fraternal joint family" would be the more appropriate term for our "family" unit.

At that time two people earned an income: Amar and Hari. Hari gave all his monthly earnings to Amar who then doled out the money according to the specific needs (not "wants") of all family members. The household budget worked on a redistributive system. I used to get five rupees for the bike pass at the railway bike stand, fifteen rupees for a second class train pass for Ghaziabad, and ten rupees as my monthly pocket money. It was tough to manage, but manage I did. During his visits to Delhi, Baoji would give me some money that helped. I am sure he did that to all of his sons. He would also bring mangoes (in season), *ghee* (purified butter), *khoa* and other goodies that Bhabhi much appreciated. He would drink in Delhi too. But he was asked to keep a leash on his loud yelling after getting drunk. He always stayed in the middle room, with Amma if she had come for a visit too, or alone. One could see the anguish on his face whenever he visited Delhi. He did not appreciate being subjected to Amar's authority.

Pretty soon life came to a routine. I was the first to leave the flat; also the first to return. A large number of students, probably in the same situation as myself, commuted to Ghaziabad to attend M.M.H. College. I made friends with many of them. Two of them stood out: Om Prakash Gupta whose father ran a business in Kuncha Ghasiram near Fatehpuri ; and Virendra Kumar Gupta whose father worked in the Delhi Cloth Mill. Both of them were brilliant students and both wanted to become engineers. Our close friendship lasted two years, although I ran into Om Prakash again in 1965 at Cornell University in U.S.A. where both of us went to do our Ph.D.s, albeit in different fields. Among the three of us, Virendra came from the poorest family. His father had seven children, six of them girls. Virendra was the oldest. But he couldn't even afford a pair of woolen pants for the cold winters and wore a pair of cotton pajama all year round. But in academics, he was the best of all three.

I became an avid movie-goer in Delhi, seeing at least one movie a week. Cinema tickets were more expensive in Delhi compared to Hapur. The cheapest ticket was one rupee 25 paisa. India went metric in 1957. The distance was now measured in kilometer, weight in kilograms, and the Indian rupee was worth 100 paisa. I liked the metric system and the new notes and coins. They symbolized independent India in a strong symbolic way. I was very fond of older movies that I had missed out on by living in smaller places. Dilip Kumar, Dev Anand, Raj Kapur, Madhubala, Nutan, Meena Kumari, Nargis, Nimmi, Nalini Jaywant, and several others were artists I liked. I started seeing their films that I had missed in special Sunday morning shows or 12 noon shows anywhere and everywhere in Delhi. The bicycle was my vehicle and I had the energy to bike to any part of the city to see those movies many of which were shown at reduced prices. That is how I became a movie buff. Dilip Kumar's *Devdas* was. and still is, one of my most favourite movies. I have seen it close to 40 times. I know each and every dialogue in this film. They don't make movies like that any more. I also admired Dilip Kumar's *Jogan, Andaaz, Shaheed, Shikast, Daag, Deedar, Amar, Naya Daur, Footpath*, and several others. I saw several of Dev Anand's older movies, like *Raahi, Munimji, Baadbaan, Taxi Driver, House No. 44, C.I.D., Funtoosh*, etc.; Raj Kapur's *Barsaat, Aag, Awara, Shri 420, Chori Chori,, Jagte Raho*, etc., and Guru Dutt's *Aar Paar* and *Mr. and Mrs. 55*. I also saw Madhubala's *Mahal, Tarana, Sangdil*, and several others, and

Balraj Sahni's *Do Bigha Zamin* and *Garam Coat*, as well as Ashok Kumar's *Achchut Kanya*, *Sangram*, and *Samadhi*. I was desperate to catch up. But watching all these movies did not jeopardize my studies. Everyone in the family, including Baoji, knew that I saw a lot of movies. But so did others, especially Amar.

I used to write letters to Baoji to keep him apprised of my studies and the happenings in Delhi. Baoji also wrote letters to me on postcards, or railway stationery sealed in an envelope. For whatever reason, I was still his favourite son; it was possibly because I was always very respectful towards him and had spent more sustained amount of time with him. His own life had become rather lonely. The nest was almost empty; only Karuna was still with Baoji and Amma. The tension between Baoji and Amar was increasing. The telltale sign of it came to the forefront every time he visited Delhi. There were increasing signs of tension between Amma and Bhabhi. The latter had changed a fair bit, had become an expert cook, and was getting more vocal and assertive. Even I noticed this transformation in her. Of course, she had full support of Amar in her deprecating behavior towards Amma. And, then, out of the blue, Karuna expressed her desire to move to Delhi herself. This devastated Baoji and Amma. Baoji began to drink even more heavily and his arguments with Amma picked up more steam. I used to learn about it

Karuna did her high school privately. She passed but with poor marks. She also did a course for a diploma in Hindi called Prabhakar. Hari, in the meantime was getting more idealistic in his outlook. Working with the customs department did not appease him. All of his colleagues at the Mathura Road office were bribe takers. In fact, if he wanted Hari could make a lot of money by doing favours to the clients whose foreign parcels he could release sooner. As a reward, gifts will come to the house: several pieces of suit materials, Swiss watches, dozens of underwear and undershirts, and so on. Hari's conscience began to hurt. To everyone's surprise, he resigned from his job. Amar was furious at him. He resigned in 1958. On his request, Baoji arranged for an all India train pass for him to travel the country. He was gone for six months. He traveled all over India, saw all parts of it, and did *pad yatra* (foot travel) to hundreds of villages in different regions of India. Surprisingly, he wrote letters to only Baoji and me. This brought me even closer to him. In 1958 Hari also started writing short stories in Hindi many of which were published in prominent weekly and monthly magazines. This made Baoji very happy. In fact, all the brothers were happy. He got paid for published stories.

Amar completed his National Diploma in Fine Arts in 1959. He immediately got a job as an Art teacher at the highly prestigious Ludlow Castle School at Kashmiri Gate. His salary also went up. He bought a Lambretta scooter and sold his bicycle. Rajeev also graduated with a bachelor of architecture degree from Delhi Polytechnic. He was immediately hired by Kanvinde and Rai, the famous architect firm in Cannaught Place. But the tension between Baoji and Amar, and between Amma and Bhabhi did not abate. Every time they came to visit in Delhi, I felt that they did not receive any respect. In fact they felt, and I agreed, that they were being insulted. Such a situation took a toll on me, especially my mental health. I realized much later in my life, that at the time I underwent serious unipolar depression. My studies began to suffer in the final year of B.Sc, at Ghaziabad. I became suicidal and made many attempts at ending my life. Of course, I did not receive any professional help. I tried to jump from the top storey of Qutb Minar, but could not do it. One day I stole a large bottle of chloroform from the chemistry laboratory of the M.M.H. College in Ghaziabad and took a train to Delhi. I pulled the train chain to stop the train before the Hindon River and immediately jumped off the train. Nobody found out who pulled the chain and stopped the train. I took out a handkerchief from my pocket, toally soaked it in chloroform, and put it on my nose. I became unconscious. I was hoping to die, but that did not happen. When I came to, it was dark all around. Slowly getting up, I walked to the next train station, took the train to Delhi, and biked home. Nobody knew what I had done.

Hari was back from his trip all over India. He had lost a lot of weight and had become extremely dark in complexion due to so much walking in the sun. He then went on a two day experiment to determine what it meant to be a coolie at the Delhi railway station. He dressed up as a coolie in red shirt and a dhoti and got a license for being a coolie He found that a coolie's life was a hard one and that if he were to take it as his profession he would not succeed. He disrobed himself from the coolie's uniform. However, a bad news came about Baoji. He was suspended from his job in Balawali. He appealed the suspension and while the hearings were going on, he came to Delhi with Amma having sold the cow, and moved all household belongings to Bawal.. But coming to Delhi was a bad idea. The taunts and bickering within the family kept going on. One day when Baoji was attending his appeal hearings in the Northern Railway office along with his defense council, Amma was kicked out of the house by Amar at Bhabhi's provocation. When Baoji came home and learned about what had happened he was furious, took his belongings and left for Bawal.

This was by no means a happy time. Another sad event further exacerbated the situation. Hari came down with pleurisy, the first stage of pleurisy where water accumulates in the lungs. It was serious. He underwent treatment for it from Dr. Sikand in Daryaganj. The treatment was expensive. Hari was unemployed. He had to face a barrage of taunts from both Amar and Bhabhi. It took Hari several months to regain his health. During this time he wrote many short stories in Hindi, including one titled *"Ek Bekar Aadmi"* ("An Unemployed Man"), that brought him repute as a story writer. This was followed by *"Mitti Ki Loth"* ("A Handful of Dirt"). Good news came that Baoji's appeal was successful and he was reinstated, but with a demotion to assistant station master level. He was posted at Makhi, a small railway station near Unnao, east of Kanpur in Uttar Pradesh. It was not the best outcome, but considering the humiliation he had undergone, he took the posting and moved there with Amma in 1959.

In 1958. Hari got a break himself. He wanted to do a Master's degree in Social Work at the Delhi School of Social Work. His B.A. degree marks were poor. On academics alone, he could not be admitted. But his travels through India, his social networking, his idealism, and the support from Hindi writers finally worked in his favour. Dr. Ranade, the school principal admitted him to the M.S.W. program. Hari was thrilled. As it turned out, he topped the school and was hired as a lecturer at the Delhi School of Social Work immediately upon graduation. This was an unprecedented feat in the history of the school. Baoji was also very happy. But my mental condition was still unsteady as I fought depression.

10

RUNNING AWAY TO CALCUTTA

It was the month of February in 1959. I was still fighting what I now know was a bout of depression. I was still suicidal. No one in the family knew about it. Nor did any of my friends. Amma came for a visit to Delhi. She came alone and stayed in the middle room. She stayed for a few days. Although I was going to my college in Ghaziabad regularly my heart was not totally in it. My visits to cinema halls had also been reduced. One day I went to the bedroom in the middle. I had seen Amma put money inside her book of Ramayana. I was wearing my only woolen suit. I took a small overnight bag. Inside the bag, I put my two- piece night pajama, a shirt, one underwear and a *banyan* (undershirt), a toothbrush and small toothpaste, the case for my eye glasses, and a *loyi* (light blanket). I stole six ten rupee notes from Amma's Ramayan, and walked out swiftly from the house. I did not take my bike. Instead I took a *tonga* (horse buggy) to the interstate bus station. I also had some of my own money, about twenty rupees. So I had close to 80 rupees with me. I took a bus to Hapur, reaching there in about an hour and a half. From the bus stop I went to the house of Buddhi, my high school buddy. I told him that I had run away from the house.

Buddhi was mad at me. He said that it was a bad idea to run away from the house. I asked him to join me in my escapade. He refused, took my hands and along with my bag took me to the bus stand, bought me a ticket for Delhi and forced me to sit inside the bus, urging me to go straight to my home. He had started working with his father and was getting late for his father's shop. He left. The bus had not yet moved from Hapur. After Buddhi was gone for two minutes, I got off the bus with my bag and took a rickshaw to the Hapur railway station. At the station I bought a third class ticket for Lucknow to travel by Sealdah Express. You see, I was only too familiar with the trains.

I was on my way to Lucknow (the capital of Uttar Pradesh) and reached there around 6:30 in the evening. I got off the train and came out of the station gate. I quickly thought that Lucknow was not the right place for me. Too many people would know or recognize me. I would be found quickly. I quickly went to the ticket window and bought a third class ticket for Sealdah and sat back in the train. I even went back to the same compartment in which I had traveled from Delhi. I bought four *puris* and *aloo sabzi* that I ate in the train. The train left the Lucknow station. For a long time I could not sleep, wondering what might have been happening in Roop Nagar when I did not return home that night. What would they do? Go to the police? Put an advertisement in the newspaper with my picture, saying that a boy named Bairaagi Sharma was missing and whoever had any information about him to please contact a given phone number. Would they beat me if I were to return? Who would they ask among my friends? Was I wrong in running away from home? Amma would certainly have found out that I had taken her money. I also thought: Everyone took me for granted: Bairaagi do this, do that. Never asked him what he wanted. Now cry for me at least until I returned. Or, may be I would not return after all. Why did I run away if I planned on returning? How about killing myself? I tossed and turned for hours, changed into the pajamas, and didn't know when I fell asleep. When I got up, it was morning. The train was entering the railway yard of Mughalsarai. Allahabad and Varanasi were left behind.

I got off the train at Mughalsarai railway station platform, washed my face, brushed my teeth and changed into my suit once again. Mughalsarai, in the state of Uttar Pradesh, was one of the largest junctions in Indian railroad network and, thus one of the busiest. I bought a cup of tea in *a kulhar* (earthen cup) and two biscuits, and had a small breakfast. The brooding mood returned again.

I decided to postpone any further decision on the next step to be taken until I reached Calcutta. In the meantime, I said to myself that I must enjoy the scenery outside as I had never been in this part of India. The train had crossed over into the state of West Bengal and was moving fast through lush green landscape consisting of paddy field and mango trees. Men and some women were working in the fields. Sometimes the train would slow down, and then would catch up speed again. It was the first time I saw houses that had ceramic tiles and gabled roof. I knew it rained hard in the region and such roofs allowed for quick dispersal of water and better drainage. The train reached Asansol, West Bengal's second largest city after Calcutta.

Asansol was situated in Burdwan district. Calcutta had two train stations, Sealdah and Howrah. The Ganga River became known as Hoogly in the area before it drained into the Bay of Bengal. It was a very pretty and picturesque setting. Next came Burdwan station itself. Finally, the train pulled into the Sealdah train station around 8 pm. I did not know a soul in the city and did not know what to do. Since the night had fallen and it was still winter, I decided to stay in the large *musafirkhana* (a large area where passengers waited for trains). I quickly went out, had some rice and *daal*, and a couple of rasgullas (a typically Bengali sweet dish) for dissert and returned to the *musafirkhana*. There were benches there. I occupied a part of one bench and slept on it. I used my bag as a pillow and *loyi* as a blanket.

Getting up early in the morning the next day, I first took care of my bodily needs under the Howrah Bridge. The bridge was an engineering feat. I looked at it for several minutes. I saw a lot of people bathing themselves in the river. It was almost 8 o'clock in the morning. I decided to go into the water. Suddenly the thought came in my head: why don't I end my life here? I took all my clothes off except the underwear, and put my shoes, clothes, glasses and leftover money in the bag. Leaving the bag near one of the *ghats*, I started slowly walking into the river. The water got deeper until it reached my chin, my mouth and then the nose. I had to take only one more step and I would have drowned to death. I stood there for almost five minutes, now shivering. But I could not take the final step. I just could not. I felt defeated, turned around, walked back to the *ghat*. There I sat, with tears in my eyes, utterly helpless with nobody knowing about what I was just attempting to do. The sun was out, and in about one hour my underwear dried up. I learned that killing oneself was one of the most difficult things to do, and I was not capable of doing that.

I dressed up and walked away from the river. What to do next? Committing suicide was not an option. Should I return home, I asked myself. People would make fun of me. The family members would be furious. Could I stay in Calcutta and make a life there? I had heard about the Ramakrishna Mission. It was located in Bolpur, accessible by bus. I decided to take the bus, bought the ticket for 50 paise and reached there in forty minutes. I told the Mission people that I had lost all my money, that somebody had picked my pocket. I asked them to give me a job; any job. The Ramakrishna Mission people figured out almost immediately that I was a runaway kid, and that I was lying about having my pocket picked. They instructed me politely to go home. They gave me ten rupees for the return journey, which was not enough.

I decided to return to Delhi. But since I did not have enough money to buy a ticket and would have had to travel without ticket anyway, I decided to treat myself with the leftover money plus what I had received from the Ramakrishna Mission. It was already 2:30 in the afternoon. I ate *Roti* and *sabzi* in a roadside restaurant, and then walked to the nearby cinema hall. The film *Sharabi* was running, starring Dev Anand and Madhubala. I watched the matinee show. After a long time, I really enjoyed watching a movie. Seeing a movie was cathartic. I was happy after resolving to return home without ticket. I walked back to the Sealdah railway station and once again spent the night at the *musafirkhana*.

Next morning, I went aboard the Sealdah-Delhi Express. Having boarded the train, I was afraid that I would be taken off the train any time for traveling without ticket. I had never traveled without ticket or train pass. Even though I was the son of a railway employee, my heart was pounding hard. I was not wrong. A ticket collector entered the train at Burdwan railway station. I again gave him the same story that my pocket had been picked, that I was the son of a railway stationmaster and that I would pay the fare once I reached my destination. The young Bengali ticket collector asked me to get off the train. I pleaded with him, but to no avail. I was pretty despondent. It was the middle of the night. The train started moving. Suddenly the ticket collector changed his mind. He nodded at me and said: "Go ahead, good luck to you." I was in tears and hugged the Bengali fellow and jumped on the train.

The rest of the journey was uneventful. I began to think what to do next. Suddenly I remembered that my grandfather's younger brother, Baba Raghubar Dayal, was posted at Tundla station that was not too far from Ghaziabad and Delhi. I made a quick decision to get off the train at Tundla station. It was a few minutes before 4 o'clock in the morning. I walked to the station office and told the assistant station master on duty that I was the grandson of Raghubar Dayalji. A porter was sent to take me to the house. It was dark and foggy. The porter took a lantern with him. He knocked at the door several times. Finally Dadi came out. They were very shocked to see me at that hour of the day but were happy to see me after a long time. I slept for about five hours quit comfortably in a bed. Got up in the morning, had breakfast, took a bath, and then got ready. Babaji bought me a ticket for Delhi for Upper India Express that left Tundla early in the afternoon. He also gave me twenty rupees. I got off the train at Ghaziabad and went to the campus of M.M.H. College to check out the B.Sc. final examination schedule.

My six examination papers were slotted between April 2 and April 18, 1959. I got a bit uptight as there was not much time left before the finals. I took a rickshaw to the bus stand in Ghaziabad and took a bus for Delhi. It was already 6:30 pm when I reached Delhi. From the bus station I walked to the home of Om Prakash Gupta. He was eating supper. He got up immediately, held my hand and came out with me to Fatehpuri. We got up on a tonga that took us to Ghantaghar. Om Prakash was quiet. He asked me where I had gone and told me that Rajeev had come looking for me to his house and that everyone in my family was were sad about my disappearance. He didn't let my hand go as we walked together to the Roop Nagar house. My three brothers were eating supper. They all got up and hugged me. No one was angry at me. Baoji and Amma were in the middle room. They too hugged me. Baoji also did not say anything; he asked me to change clothes and eat supper.

I went to bed early. I only said that I had gone to Calcutta and spent the last night with Baba and Dadi in Tundla, had stopped over in Ghaziabad to check the examination schedule before coming to Delhi. I was not asked why I ran away. Amma also did not chastise me for stealing money from her Ramayan. Hari told me that I would be going to watch the cricket test match between India and the visiting West Indies team that was to start the next day. I was all excited. Next day was a Sunday, and all four brothers went to the Feroz Shah Kotla cricket grounds near Delhi Gate. In 1959 the West Indies team was all powerful with the pace battery of Roy Gilchrist and Wesley Hall, the batsmen of the caliber of Garfield Sobers, Rohan Kanhai, and Frank Worrell. India had opening batsmen in Nari Contractor and Pankaj Roy, the big name batsmen in Vijay Merchant, Vijay Hazare, and G. S. Ramchand, allrounder Vinoo Mankad, and an upcoming speedster in Ramakant Desai. It was an entertaining match and ended in a draw. I watched the match live on four of the five days. I had never seen a live cricket match where countries competed for test matches before this.

Hari took me to a Bungalow Road café one day and asked me what prompted me to leave the house and go to Calcutta. I could not open up to him. But I promised that I would write about it and give it to him soon. I kept my promise. It took me a few days to put my thoughts together to explain to Hari what had bothered and upset me and caused me to think negatively. In those days the word depression was not in the vocabulary of everyday parlance. The write-up was 11 pages long. Having read it, Hari Bhai told me that I had every reason to feel that way. He hugged me tightly. I cried hard. non-stop for several minutes. It was extremely therapeutic for me. Life began to return to a new normal again.

11

GHAZIABAD, DELHI, AND RAJEEV'S WEDDING

I passed and graduated with a high second division in B.Sc. I attended my convocation at M.M.H. College. The experience was such that I never felt like attending another convocation. The keynote speaker for the convocation was India's defense minister, V. K. Krishna Menon. This man had a record for speaking in the United Nations on the Kashmir issue in 1948. He was in his elements in Ghaziabad too. He spoke for one hour and forty-five minutes, boring everybody to death. Not a great experience for the graduates. Once again, I could not apply to Delhi University for a Master's program because I was not 19 years old. So it was decided that I continue studying at M.M.H. College, Ghaziabad for a M.Sc. degree in Mathematics. I was sharp in mathematics and began to enjoy my classes. I also got an opportunity to apply for a position of Demonstrator/Junior Lecturer in Physics in the Intermediate College. I got the position that provided me a salary of 290 rupees a month. I was happy, but most of all it was Baoji who felt proud of his youngest son beginning to earn at the age of 17.

Amar became very fascinated by North Indian (Hindustani) classical music. He decided to learn how to play the sitar. He bought a sitar from

Rikhi Ram & Sons, a reputed store for musical instruments located on Nai Sadak in old Delhi. He tried to play the instrument on his own at the Rohtak Road flat. Then things got busy with Babboo's birth and the move to Roop Nagar. He found a good teacher in Zamaluddin Bharati who lived in Kamla Nagar. Amar needed table accompaniment and he roped me in to learn playing the table. This was soon after I had moved to Delhi in 1957 and had started commuting to Ghaziabad for my B.Sc. studies. A pair of tabla was bought for me, also from Nai Sadak. An old man, named Gopal Sharma, instructed me in playing tabla. Despite his old age he came by bicycle from Fatehpuri three times a week. He was a very good teacher and taught me all the *talas* (beat cycles). I learned Dadra taal (6 beats), Keharwa taal (8 beats), Jhap taal (10 beats), Roopak taal (7 beats), Ek taal (10 beats), and Teen taal (16 beats). The emphasis was placed on Ek taal, Roopak taal, Jhap taal, and Teen taal. He also taught me some *tukras*, in *drut* taal (fast beat).

In accompanying Amar, I acquired some knowledge of classical *ragas*. Gradually this interest began to turn into a passion. I listened to a good deal of classical music and began to relate to the specific combination of notes that characterize a raga. The radio in the house was tuned only to Delhi A station that played mostly classical music. Radio Ceylon and later Vividh Bharati stations were rarely tuned in, only when Amar was not around. This caused some resentment among other family members who were not fans of classical music. This interest in north Indian classical music has survived for me to this day and Amar was responsible for it during my teenage years.

He and I attended several national programs of classical music at Akashvani Bhavan in New Delhi, featuring big name artists like Ustad Bade Ghulam Ali Khan, Kumar Gandharva, Ustad Bismillah Khan, Gajanan Rao Joshi, Pannalal Ghosh, Vilayat Khan, Ali Akbar Khan, Siddheshwari Devi, Pt. Onkar Nath Thakur, Pt. Bhimsen Joshi, and many more.

I also attended a number of classical concerts. I remember one by Ustad Ali Akbar Khan on the Sarod playing an afternoon raga called Madhuvanti at Max Muller Bhavan in New Delhi. I was simply enchanted. Khan Sahib remained my favourite artist until his death recently. One evening I went to attend a vocal concert by Bade Ghulam Ali Khan at Sapru House. After the concert was over, I walked to the stage, and said to Khan Sahib that I was a novice at listening to classical music, but I liked his singing a lot for it had a sweet mesmerizing effect on me. Khan Sahib complimented me on my interest in classical music. When I asked him how long he did riyaz (practice), he said "five to six hours a day aside from teaching his pupils. When asked how he cultivated such melodious voice, he gave an interesting answer: *"Beta, yeh jo mera bada sa pait hai, yeh ek matka hai aur isme neeche tak sur bhare pade hain; oon suron ko mein khench khench kar nikalta hoon"* ("Son, in this big tummy of mine, resembling a big earthen pitcher, the musical notes are hidden right to the bottom and in my singing I pull them out one after the other."). We both laughed loudly, as did his son Munnawar Ali who was giving him vocal support. Over the years from 1957 to 1965, I had the opportunity to listen live to so many accomplished classical artists. Among my favourites were: Nikhil Bannerji, Ustad Amir Khan, Pandit

Bhimsen Joshi, Kumar Gandharva, Nazakat Ali Salamat Ali, and the older Dagar Brothers, Nasir Aminuddin and Nasir Moinuddin.

But my fascination with Hindi films continued. From April 2, 1959 to April 20, 1959, while writing the B.Sc. final examinations I saw 10 films. I did not believe in rote learning. Especially during the examination period, I believed in relaxing as much as possible. This spate of ten films was despite my running away to Calcutta just a bit more than a month earlier. I used to keep an immaculate diary in which I will enter every film I saw, the title of the film, the date it was seen, the show timing, and the theatre where I saw it. This diary often landed me in a lot of trouble from Amar. But he too kept a similar diary of films he saw. In fact, I borrowed the idea of keeping a diary from him. I remember one day on a winter evening in 1959 I was parking my bike at the Regal cinema in Cannaught Place for the 6pm to 9 pm show. I saw Amar at the bike stand. He was picking up his bike after watching the matinee show of the same film. He asked me what I was doing there. I asked him the same question. He smiled and said; 'don't tell your Bhabhi (sister-in-law) that you saw me here". I smiled too and nodded my head.

One of the ten films I saw in April 1959 was *Chhoti Behan*, a tear jerker. I had an exam in Ghaziabad from 2:00 to 5:00 pm. Rather than return home directly upon reaching Delhi I biked to Palace Cinema near Sabzi Mandi and saw the evening show. It ended at 9:00 pm. I had cried a lot in this film that starred Balraj Sahni and Nanda. My eyes were red with crying. My brothers were eating supper and I joined them after washing my hands. Looking at me they all thought that I had bombed in the exam.

I had a tough time convincing them that that was not the case. Baoji was visiting Delhi for a couple of days. He had seen the movie the day before. His comment about Balraj Sahni was: *"Sala, bada jajbati actor hai"* ("That son of a gun is a really emotional actor".)

I greatly enjoyed working as a Demonstrator in the Physics Laboratory at the Intermediate College component of M.M.H. College. I had to dress up for the job, shirt, tie and all. This gave me a sense of authority and it enhanced my self-image. Whenever Baoji visited Delhi, he looked at me appreciatively. Whenever he visited Delhi during wintertime, he slept in the corner room on Hari's bed. He asked me what I did with my salary. I responded that I handed over every penny of it to Amar.

"How much does your Bhai Sahib give you for pocket money every month?'

"Fifteen rupees," I replied.

"That's it? How do you manage with your fondness for movies"?

"I "I manage somehow".

Since I left very early in the morning, I used to hang my clothes on a hanger above the cot where I slept. That morning Baoji said he would come with me as he had to go to Moradabad by Sealdah Express, the train I took to Ghaziabad every morning. He and I went to the railway station in a three-wheeler scooter. It felt good not having to bicycle for a change. Baoji insisted that I sit with him in a first class compartment, rather than the usual second class I used everyday. The train ran a bit late that morning. I touched Baoji's feet and got off at the Ghaziabad platform. Baoji blessed me and asked me to take a rickshaw to reach the college on time. As I was about to walk, Baoji said,"*Apni jeb ka dhyan rakhna*" ("Take care of your pocket"). I took a rickshaw. And then suddenly remembered what Baoji had said about taking care of the pocket. I slipped my hand inside the inner pocket of my suit jacket. It had two one hundred rupee notes inside it. I started crying. It was one of those tender actions that I never forgot about my father.

During my tenure as a Demonstrator in the Physics department at M.M.H. College I found a very good friend in a lecturer in English. His name was K. L. Sharma. He was well above six feet tall and handsome. His father had passed away when he was just one year old, and her mother alone had raised and educated him. Like me, K. L. Sharma also biked to the train station in Delhi. We traveled in the same compartment everyday. Once he invited me to his house to meet his mother in a one-room accommodation in Karol Bagh. Her mother was a very pretty, tall, and kind lady. The mother and son had come to India as refugees from Pakistan at the time of India's partition in 1947. They underwent much hardship as refugees. Both K.L. and I were fond of movies and saw a number of them together. We also went to coffee houses in Cannaught Place several times and listened to our favourite songs at the jukebox. It cost 25 paisas to play a song. We also did boating at the canal near India Gate a few times. K.L. Sharma had become my closest friend.

Baoji was suspended in 1958 while he was posted at Balawali. This was due to the corruption charges laid against him while he worked in Simbhaoli. The period of suspension was a down time for Baoji. But he was a fighter and, through legal counsel and several hearings, he was reinstated, but as assistant stationmaster in Makhi. He retired in 1959. It was his belief that he would live with his sons. Amar and Bhabhi would not go for it and there was a lot of tension and acrimony for the brief period of two months he stayed in Delhi. Baoji and Amma decided to move to Bawal with all their belongings. But Baoji didn't like staying in Bawal doing nothing. In 1960 he was offered a three-year extension to his job. Baoji took the extension and he was once again posted at Makhi for a period of three years. The extension was to last till December end in 1963.

Makhi was a very small railway station near Unnao, about 50 km east of Kanpur. He did not like the place but he did not have any other options. The relationship between Baoji and Amar had become much strained and while Hari, Rajeev, Karuna, and I visited Amma and Baoji in Makhi, Amar and Bhabhi never did. After moving to Delhi in 1957, I became very attached to my infant nephew< Babboo. I learned from Bhabhi how diapers were put on a male child. Soon after coming back from Ghaziabad, I used to change Babboo's cloth diaper, dress him up, put talcum powder on his face and neck and take him for a walk in his walker. Our walking route took us to less crowded Bungalow Road going past Kirorimal College and the coffee house and then return home. Kids were always dear to me and I bonded well with them. Babboo got so used to this routine that he would cry his heart out if I were to get late in taking him out.

Around the middle of 1959, Babaji (my grandfather) began to put pressure on Baoji for getting another one of his grandsons married before he were to pass away. Baoji talked to Hari and discussed this matter with Amar also through letters. But Hari was not ready to marry yet since his career was still not quite where he wanted it to be. He told Baoji to go ahead and negotiate a marriage for Rajeev who already had a good job. So the focus of matrimonial pressure shifted on Rajeev and he seemed to be willing to get married. Baoji had a friend, named Hira Lal Sharma, in the railway hierarchy who was in a senior position as well as older than Baoji. He had once shown interest in Hari as a prospective groom for his youngest daughter who was a student at Miranda College at Delhi University and was soon to graduate with a B.A. degree. Baoji told his friend about Hari's unwillingness to marry at that time, but intimated him about Rajeev being ready for matrimony. Hira Lalji seemed quite keen to pursue this.

Mr. Hira Lal Sharma had lost his wife shortly after the birth of their last child. His family consisted of two sons and three daughters. The oldest was a son, named Mool Raj who was a naval officer and married to Shakuntala Devi. Three daughters came next, named Raj (a very successful gynecologist) who was married to Ram Gaur, Mohini married to Shiv Kumar, and Saloni, the new bride to be. The youngest child was a son named Gyan who was going to medical school. This was a prosperous family with domestic help, servants, and an armed force culture that emphasized hierarchy, discipline and etiquette. In the late summer of 1959 Mool Raj and his wife came to meet Rajeev and to present the marriage proposal to Amar. They brought with them a black and white photograph of Saloni. The photograph reminded me of the well-known Hindi film actress, Geetabali, who was very popular in the 1950s. All went well in this meeting and the path was cleared for the marriage ceremony. It was agreed that Rajeev and Saloni could meet and spend time together alone to get to know each other.

I called Rajeev at his office and took a bus to Cannaught Place to meet him. I informed him how everybody liked Saloni's picture. Rajeev was very happy and treated me with a milkshake at the Wengers restaurant. Rajeev and Saloni dated often. Their marriage was fixed for February 28, 1960.

Good times and bad times in family dynamics often draw people together. This could be said quite appropriately about Rajeev's marriage. Preparations were on full swing on both bride and groom's sides. I had not yet met Saloni and was anxious to have an opportunity to see her. I made this opportunity in my own somewhat childish manner. Like in Simbhaoli, I took to cricket in Ghaziabad as well and was elected to the college team. I remember one match against Deshbandhu College in Kalkaji. We won that match handily. I had an all-round performance, scoring 65 runs before getting out caught close to the long on boundary, and I took four wickets for 27 runs. That day I also ate meat for the first time in my life. While eating lunch in Kalkaji during the match, I ate two small bowls of mutton curry thinking it was *Masoor daal*. Obviously, I liked it a lot.

There was a picnic planned for the college cricket team in Okhla for a Sunday afternoon. Baoji was visiting Delhi briefly. He had brought with him his handsome gramaphone that had a brown leather exterior and looked like a fashionable briefcase when closed. The gramophone needed some service and adjustment and I got it done at Maharaja Lal & Sons. While at the shop, I also bought a 78 rpm record of my favourite film Devdas. Both songs were sung by Lata Mangeshkar; *"Jise tu kabool karle woh adaa kahan se laoon"* and *"O janewale rookja koi dam"*. I decided to take the gramophone to the picnic, with this and many other records, as well as a pack of playing cards. I took a bus to Okhla, along with my food cooked by Bhabhi, *aloo paranthas* (shallow fried chapatti stuffed with potatoes) and home made lime pickle. I reached Okhla picnic spot at 3 pm. But there was no one there; no other member of the team came for the picnic. I was hugely disappointed. Having walked for about half an hour on the banks of the Yamuna River, I got hungry; so I ate the *paranthas*. Having rested for a while, I decided to return home. I took a bus that brought me to India Gate. I needed to change the bus to go to Roop Nagar.

Suddenly I remembered that Saloni's brother, Mool Raj Sharma, and his family lived close by at the Princess Park Mess. I decided to go there for a visit. Of course, nobody expected me to drop in like that. There were only women present there: Saloni, her older sister, Shyam, Saloni's Bhabhi, Shakuntala Devi, and latter's younger sister, Rani. There were a lot of jokes and laughter. I played the record from Devdas on my gramophone which all appreciated. After some tea and snacks I left for home. This visit by me was talked about for quite some time, causing some embarrassment to me. Even Baoji didn't like my visit to Princess Park when he heard about it. He said: *"Is tarah bina bulaye nayi rishtedari me nahi jana chahiye"* ("One should not go uninvited to a new relative's house.")

Ram Kumar Chachaji was transferred from Rewari to Lahori Gate (part of Delhi). He came to Roop Nagar every once in a while. My first year in a Master's program at M.M.H. College, Ghaziabad was progressing well and I really enjoyed my job in the Physics laboratory. Students seemed to like me as they found me helpful in understanding basic concepts of physics. There was one student in the degree college who traveled by the same trains to and from Ghaziabad. I found her quite attractive and tried to make friends with her. But I did not go very far in my efforts. Our acquaintance thus did not go much beyond formal greetings. One day after college I ran into her on Nai Sadak. Both of us were there for the same purpose, buying books. We said hello to each other. But once again, she left in a hurry. I gave up trying.

The date for Rajeev's wedding was approaching. It was decided to do the *janeo* (sacred thread worn by upper caste, or so-called "twice-born" Hindus) ceremony at Roop Nagar. A priest does the *pooja* for the occasion. Janeo is done for two people at a time. So I was asked to tag along with Rajeev. We took bath, and wore fresh clothes but nothing above the waist. Baoji, Chachaji, Amma, Bhua, and all the members of family were present. Rajeev and I sat cross-legged on mats on the floor. At the conclusion of pooja, the priest gave us the janeo to wear. The ceremony was over. There are customary regulations to be followed by anyone who wears the janeo. Neither Rajeev nor I wanted to observe these regulations. So we decided to take our janeos off and tied them carefully on flower plants. Baoji, who always wore a janeo, was not very happy by our abandonment of the janeo.

From early age both Chachaji and Bhua were asthmatic. Negotiating stairs was often difficult for them and winter months were especially taxing. We usually watched out for them on this matter. Chachi was short and heavy but with a happy ambience. Both she and Chachaji derived a great deal of pleasure in partaking of rites of passage for their nephews and nieces. Thus Rajeev's wedding was a very happy occasion for them, especially given the fact that he had spent a number of years with them in Rewari. Arrangements for the wedding were in high gear and Amar was making most of the decisions with occasional consultation with Amma, Baoji, and Rajeev. It was decided to put up some of the relatives with friends. Only the closest relatives stayed in Roop Nagar. It was decided to have a traditional wedding with a marriage band, a mare for the groom, a Shehnai player, and a bus to transport the *baraat* to the bride's house.

The reception for the *baraat* was held in the large hall of the mess. Alcoholic beverages were served as well. Baoji was glowing in pride and he liked being in limelight when photographed with Saloni's family, especially the elders, her father and *Taoji* (father's older brother). After a long time I saw Baoji so happy. He had had a few drinks but he was very pleasant, good mannered, and respectful to his own father and brother. The *phere*, according to the *mahurat* (auspicious time) were scheduled for 2:30 am. Thus the final marriage ritual actually took place on February 29, 1960. Someone joked: "You will celebrate your wedding anniversary only once in four years" (in leap years).

Rajeev's wedding was a rare occasion that brought the family together. But once the festivities ended and the old routine settled in, the tranquil period was to be gradually but surely replaced by unease and turbulence. Within a week past their marriage, Rajeev and Saloni went to Nainitaal for their honeymoon. Baoji helped with the free train passes up to Kathgodam via Bareiiley. I overheard some conversation between Amar and Bhabhi to the effect that they never had a honeymoon.

At Rajeev's wedding Baoji received a suit piece in gray Lal Imli (a well known brand name) wool. Baoji said to Amma that he did not need a suit and urged me to get a suit made for myself. I was reluctant to do so but upon his persistent urging I conceded. It was a handsome suit that I wore with great pride on my job at Ghaziabad.

12

CONFLICT IN THE JOINT FAMILY

In the second year of my Master's program I lost interest in Mathematics. I found it dry and uninteresting. So I decided to quit the program. Amar did not like my decision. Baoji's response was neutral. He argued that commuting to Ghaziabad was just too taxing for me and that I would do better at Delhi University the following year. Hari graduated at the top of his class in Social Work in 1961 and was immediately hired as a lecturer, a rarity for a fresh graduate. Rajeev was still working with Kanvinde and Rai firm in Cannaught Place and seemed to be enjoying it. He played a key role in the design of the impressive campus of Indian Institute of Technology in Kanpur. But he was also exploring other possibilities for his professional career. Karuna had completed her matriculation and a Prabhakar diploma in Hindi. She was leaning towards the field of fine arts. Amar was still teaching at the Ludlow Castle School at Kashmiri Gate.

One afternoon in the summer of 1960, one middle aged woman, named Saraswati Arora, along with her young and beautiful daughter, came to visit. She told Amar that she was a music teacher at the Roop Nagar Multipurpose Higher Secondary School in the girls' section (morning shift) and that Mr. Bhushan Swami (Amma's cousin) was her colleague. She introduced the young woman as Manjari (in short, Manju). Manju was very beautiful and was wearing a skirt and a blouse. She was 17 years old, one year older than Karuna. Mrs. Arora sought Amar's advice and help in getting Manju admitted into the 5-year national diploma program in Fine Arts at the Delhi Polytechnic. Amar had completed that diploma in 1958 (he did it on a part-time basis in seven years). Amar agreed to mentor both Karuna and Manju for entrance to the Fine Arts program. He taught them some basic things, like free hand drawing straight lines and circles, colour identification and mixing, use of brushes and paint, raw materials needed, and the differences between two dimension and three dimension objects and art works. This was extremely useful training and went a long way towards the admission of both Karuna and Manju in the Fine Arts program at the Delhi Polytechnic.. Manju and Karuna became life long friends. I got to know Manju a little bit in 1961. She used to come to our flat every morning to go to join Karuna to take the bus together to Kashmiri Gate where the polytechnic was situated.. I almost never saw them in the morning since I used to leave for Ghaziabad much earlier.

Saloni was a free spirit and had a bubbly personality. She wasn't used to doing household chores. As for her culinary skills she was much like a novice. She was more into making up her face, and wearing good-looking clothes, talking and making jokes. She had a very happy and innocent demeanour. Tension began to arise between Bhabhi and her. Saloni loved to spend time outside the home, go to restaurants, watch movies, visit friends, etc., things that Bhabhi had pretty little time for. This tension found its way to Amar who took his wife's side in these matters. Like Hari and myself, Rajeev also used to hand in his salary to Amar every month, but after his marriage, Rajeev needed more money for personal expenses that Amar was reluctant to provide him.

Lack of compromise on Amar's part led to frequent arguments between Rajeev and him. Hari tried to mediate but it did not work out. One day in the heat of the argument between Rajeev and Amar, the latter lost his cool and slapped Rajeev. The latter was shocked and told Amar that he was going to move out of 2/28 Roop Nagar. It seemed that Amar was prepared for this eventuality and he pulled out a pro-note for Rajeev to sign. The pro-note had a high sum of money that Amar had allegedly spent on Rajeev's education and by signing the pro-note Rajeev was undertaking the obligation to repay that sum to Amar. There was no taking into account of the money that Rajeev had already given to Amar after he started earning, nor was account taken of help that Rajeev had provided with his talent on various projects that Amar had undertaken for exhibition grounds in New Delhi.

Rajeev signed the pro-note and in a few days moved to a bachelor's apartment in Shakti Nagar, not too far from where the rest of us lived. This was the beginning of the split within the fraternal joint family and the first time Amar felt his "patriarchal" authority being threatened. His stance vis-à-vis Rajeev was a reflection of the insecurity he had felt. Whether there was a justification for what he did was for others to interpret. But it definitely created a very tense situation for the rest of the family members. Visiting Rajeev and Saloni in Shakti Nagar could easily have been construed as being disloyal to Amar. There was special pressure on Karuna and me. We visited Shakti Nagar discreetly. However, we could sense that Amar and Bhabhi were aware of visits. But there was really not much they could do about it as long as we did not compromise our responsibilities. Baoji, Chachaji, and Bhua were conflicted too. Whenever Baoji visited Delhi, he visited both places openly without any fear of Amar. It was especially difficult for Chachaji and Bhua to visit Rajeev and Saloni as their asthmatic condition was not conducive to climbing stairs to the top (2nd floor) of the building to reach Rajeev's bachelor flat, referred to as "Barsaati" in Delhi's linguistic parlance.

Saloni and I became good friends who shared most things, i.e., news, ideas, events, happening, etc. I had once asked Rajeev if it would be okay for Saloni and I to go see a movie. He said that would be just fine. So the two of us saw a number of movies together, usually a matinee show. Baoji was generally okay with Rajeev's separation from Amar. He visited them just as often as he did folks in Roop Nagar. He felt more secure and relaxed at Rajeev's place. He often demanded what he wanted to eat on a particular evening. Of course, he drank at their place too. But I never heard Rajeev complain about Baoji making noise when he got drunk. Amma cut down on her visiting to Delhi. Whenever she came with him, she spent time visiting her uncle and his family at Mori Gate, more distant relatives in old Delhi, or visiting Bhua in Bawal or her younger sister Mini in Alwar. Amma had no fear of traveling alone.

Babaji got sick in Bawal in the early summer of 1961. He passed away that summer. Everybody went to Bawal for his last rituals. I could not go because somebody needed to be present in the flat and I was also busy with my remaining duty at M.M.H. Intermediate College in Ghaziabad. Since I did not know how to cook at the time, arrangements for my food were made in a nearby restaurant in Shakti Nagar. In the last two years of my going to Ghaziabad everyday for four years, I started smoking occasionally and quite enjoyed it. But I only bought one cigarette at a time and lighted it with a burning string on the side of the smoke shop.

In the final practical examination in Physics at the Ghaziabad College, I learned something I did not know before. The final mark in the practical section was to be decided by three people: the external examiner, the class instructor, and m as the laboratory demonstrator. The assignment of final mark began around 8 pm in the physics laboratory. There was a lot of pressure from the parents of some students to have their sons/daughters get a higher mark than they deserved. A hefty amount in bribe was offered to the three of the decision makers. I was, on moral principles, totally against this. We had an animated and heated discussion on the topic. Without reaching any decision we adjourned for dinner at 10 pm. It was a sumptuous meal, obviously made possible by the money of some parents. Resuming the meeting at 11:30 pm., the discussion went on for another three and a half hours. Despite my vehement objections many marks went substantially up. Six parents offered monies to the decision makers. I was disgusted and refused to take any money. However, I did accept a ride to my home in Delhi where I reached at 4 o'clock in the morning. This was my last act in Ghaziabad. I was left with a sour taste in my mouth.

In the summer of 1961 I found a job as a chemist in the Food Laboratory of the Municipal Corporation of Delhi. Chemistry was always my favourite subject and I really enjoyed the job that lasted for two months. It was the laboratory's mandate to test the purity of food that was marketed. There were a number of food inspectors who would go to retailers in the food market, and collect samples of all kinds of food: grains, rice, spices, tea, coffee, even cold drinks, etc. Our laboratory examination found some weird facts. We found horse excreta in turmeric; a lizard in a coca cola bottle; a razor blade in a can of jackfruit; very finely chipped stones/pebbles in many samples of lentils and other *daals*. It was a very interesting experience.

While working as a chemist, I started reading some of the social sciences books that belonged to Hari. These were books in sociology and social work, as well as a number of village studies. I was fascinated. This was far more interesting than the dry subjects of mathematics and integral calculus. An idea started creeping in my head. I wanted to do my master's program in a social science. Hari suggested that I go into anthropology that was an established discipline at Delhi University. I made up my mind and applied for admission into a master's program in anthropology. I was easily accepted into a two-year master's program.

13

DELHI UNIVERSITY

So, finally I was a student at Delhi University, having waited for this for four years. I was affiliated with Hindu College. But I went there only to deposit my fees. All the classes were held in the Faculty of Arts that housed the department. The department head was Dr. Prafulla Chandra Biswas, a physical anthropologist who was the founder member of the department since 1948. I never took any classes from him. The department had a strong orientation towards physical anthropology, with a number of faculty members: besides Dr. Biswas, Dr. Abhimanyu Sharma, Dr. Inderpal Singh Monga, Dr S.C. Tiwari, and a part-time Anatomy professor who was actually a physician/surgeon. There was no one teaching Linguistics. Dr. J. D. Mehra and Professor R.D. Sanwal taught social/cultural anthropology. Dr. Mehra, Dr. Sharma, and Dr. Tiwari taught prehistory and archaeology. There were no specific courses on applied anthropology. In the first year of the master's program, students were required to take classes in three sub-disciplines: social anthropology, physical anthropology, and archaeology. In the second (final) year students were required to specialize in either physical anthropology or social anthropology. There was a departmental library, and a museum-cum-laboratory that housed material cultural and archaeological collections from different parts of India, Africa, and Australia, as well as instruments and facilities for undertaking craniometry, somatometry, and blood-typing. In our batch there were eight students who specialized in physical anthropology in the final year, and another eight who specialized in social anthropology. I belonged to the latter group.

Among the students there was a high degree of closeness. In the female gang there was the studious Krishna Dasgupta, a very pleasant Subhashini Khullar, a bubbly Manjit Kaur, and slightly shortish Nalini Oje. Besides me, the male group consisted of Joseph Karinattu who came from Ernakulum, Kerala, a sober and generally quiet Moorthy, a friendly Mool Raj Verma, and a Haryanavi young man named Jaswant Singh Yadav who became my lifelong buddy. Joseph was a great guy. He did not speak a word of Hindi when he first came to Delhi. He lived at Jubilee Hall, one of the large male hostels of Delhi University. Many times we visited him at Jubilee Hall and ate lunch with him. I used to take four *paranthas* and some dry vegetable for my lunch, provided to me by Bhabhi. All of the guys used to grab the pieces of paranthas and they were consumed in no time. Afterwards, we would go to the coffee House on campus, and have *dosha* (a rice and *daal* crape stuffed with potatoes) and coffee. It only cost 25 paise for a cup of excellent coffee.

Jaswant was a combative fellow when I first met him, a bit aggressive, and rather quick to lose his temper. To a certain degree I had a calming influence on him. He was not very tall, but well built and strong. He had lost his mother at a very young age. He lived in a *barsaati* with his older brother,

Raj, in Rana Pratap Bagh within short walking distance from where I lived. His father would often visit. As our friendship grew we began to hang out together very frequently. We shared our happiness and sorrows. I knew then that we would be life long friends. Saloni, who I also called Bhabhi (as she was my sister-in-law), also joined Delhi University to do her master's program in Hindi. Her classes were also held in the Arts faculty although she was affiliated with Miranda College. Not infrequently we went to the university and returned home together.

Baoji did not know anything about anthropology. During one of his visits to Delhi, Hari and I explained to him what anthropology entailed. He wanted to know what the chances of employability were once I completed my program. We talked anthropology up and discussed various possibilities for employment. He sounded convinced, wished me well and asked me to communicate with him regularly. He also started sending me a money order ranging from 15 to 25 rupees every month at my department address. It was a big help coming from him to me. Amar had no knowledge of this assistance to me from Baoji. I started writing letters to him, once every week. In return, he sent me a letter every week written in well-constructed English. These letters were as much a testimony of his penmanship, as indicative of his love, affection and concern for me. I cherish those letters to this day.

Things generally went calmly. Saloni and I saw many movies together in 12 noon shows without cutting any classes. She had hard time sitting in one place for more than an hour. The main library of Delhi University used to be very crowded. So I decided to sit in the library of Shriram College of Commerce that was close by. Saloni also decided to do so. She had a close friend named Rajni. They usually sat together in the library. Quite often Saloni would coax Rajni to go for coffee at the Wenger's restaurant located next to the main library. Sometimes I joined them as well. The days on which Rajni wasn't around she would urge me to go for coffee. I usually resisted that and asked her to concentrate on studying. Besides, our frequent outings to the restaurant, and even walking together, gave the impression to some people that we were "boyfriend-girl friend". I resented that very much, but there was not much we could do about it. Sometimes we took Karuna also to see a movie with us. It was difficult to synchronize since Karuna's polytechnic was at Kashmiri Gate. So when she joined us, it was almost always at Majestic or Ritz cinema halls that were within five-minute walking distance from the polytechnic. Of course, no one at home knew about our escapades to movies.

Baoji was very fond of reading novels in both Urdu and Hindi. Munshi Prem Chand, Sa-adat Hassan Manto, Kishan Chander, and Vrindavan Lal Verma were among his favourite authors. I could check out up to 10 books at a time from Delhi University library for a period of 8 weeks. I used these facilities for borrowing books for Baoji. He was extremely happy and appreciative of having access to the novels. The month of December in 1961 was bitterly cold in northern India. The sun did not come out in Delhi at all for ten consecutive days. I decided to visit Amma and Baoji in Makhi during the Christmas break. I took the overnight Upper India Express train from

Delhi railway station to Kanpur. I had a berth in the sleeper coach. I was wearing two sweaters over an undershirt and shirt, had covered myself with a quilt and a blanket, but I was still shivering. The train reached Kanpur on time in the morning. I had to change for Unnao and again for Makhi.

The train to Unnao got delayed on the way and I missed my morning train connection to Makhi. I was not very happy with this turn of events. I went to the office of the stationmaster in Unnao to send a message to Baoji in Makhi. The next train was in the evening. Baoji asked me to take a rickshaw from Unnao to Makhi.. That was one of most difficult rickshaw rides of my life. The rickshaw puller was working hard to peddle the rickshaw; he was actually sweating despite the bitter cold. I had covered myself with a blanket and yet I was extremely cold. My nose was dripping. I had bought a pack of cigarettes in Unnao and must have smoked four or five of them during the eight kilometers journey. The porter, sent by Baoji, was waiting for me at the outer signal of Makhi. He picked up my suitcase and bedding and we walked to the railway quarter where Amma and Baoji lived. This was my second visit to Makhi.

Baoji was sitting on a cot covering himself in a blanket and was wearing a scarf on his head. There was an *angeethi* (a coal burning cooking device) next to his cot to keep him warm. I touched Baoji's feet. He embraced me and said: "*Aa gaye beta. Badi takleef huyi hogi itni thand me.*" ("You are here son. It must have been difficult in such a cold weather"). I touched Amma's feet as well. She was very happy to see me. I washed my face and once again brushed my teeth. Amma brought freshly made *aloo paranthas* for me for breakfast and a hot cup of tea. We exchanged news. Both Amma and Baoji were anxious to know about everybody. They were especially worried about Karuna. I told her that she was doing fine. They also asked me if I visited Rajeev and Saloni, and I affirmed that. He asked about Chachaji's asthma and urged me to visit him as often as I could. I had brought eight books from the library for Baoji. His eyes brightened up. He put on his reading glasses and started turning the pages of the books. For Amma I had brought a shawl that Rajeev had bought for her. She had a smile on her face.

I asked Baoji about his health. Somehow he looked thinner to me. He responded by saying that he had been having some difficulty in swallowing food. I urged him to get a check up from the railway doctor in Unnao. Baoji indicated that he was planning to go to Moradabad and would have himself examined there at the railway hospital. That put my mind to rest. Baoji had night duty that day starting at midnight. He had a two-hour nap in the afternoon after a good lunch prepared by Amma. I also had a nap. In the evening Baoji drank a fair amount and suddenly asked me:

"*Woh tera bhaisahib kaisa hai? Sharam nahin ayee apne jawan bhai per haat uthate huye.*" ("How is your oldest brother? He wasn't ashamed of hitting his grown up brother").

"*Saala Kutta, mere samne karta to uska mhoo tod deta*" ("Scoundrel, dog, if he had dared to do it in my presence, I would have broken his face").

I tried to calm him down:

> *"Chhodiye Baoji, aap kyon pareshan hote hein. Shayad yeh
> hona hi tha. Ho gaya to theek hi hai. Apne apne ghar mein
> dono khush hein"* ("Please, let go Baoji. Why do you make
> yourself unhappy? Perhaps this was bound to happen. It's
> okay now that it happened. Both are happy in their own
> houses.")

Amma also wanted to add fuel to the fire, but I stopped her from doing so. Baoji ate his food and after rinsing his mouth and teeth, he went to sleep for another two hours. We woke him up just before midnight and he went to the station to do his night shift.

I woke up late next morning. Baoji had come back home from his duty and was reading the newspaper that came by the morning train from Unnao. After a cup of hot tea, I dressed myself warmly and with a *lota* (round shaped metal tumbler) full of water I went out to relieve myself out in the fields. It was still very cold and there was no sign of the sun coming out. I walked on narrow paths in the fields of mustard and wheat. There were also fields of vegetables such as peas and chickpeas. Although it was cold, the fields looked beautiful. At some distance there were mango and guava trees that bore fruit in summer time after the monsoon rains. I rested that day and told Baoji that I would make a day trip to Kanpur the next day to see a movie.

The trip to Kanpur was enjoyable. I bought two 78 rpm records. One was by my favourite singer, Talat Mahmood, and the other by K.L. Saigal, Baoji's favourite singer. I also bought a fresh box of needles used to play records on the gramophone. Talat's record had the memorable songs "*Shame gham ki kasam*" and "*Mein pagal mera manua pagal*". Saigals's record had the two famous *ghazals*: "*Aye qatibe tadbeer mujhe itna batade*" and "*Nukta chin hai ghame dil*". The film "Hum Dono" was also excellent, one of Dev Anand's very best. I also bought some sweets for Amma and Baoji. I was back in Makhi at supper time. It was a Tuesday, so Baoji did not drink for he was fasting for *Hanumanji*. It was a nice evening, with excellent meal prepared by Amma, followed by sweets I brought from Kanpur for dissert. I was tired, so went to bed early. Before going to bed I told Amma and Baoji that I would be leaving on Thursday evening. They were not happy as they expected me to stay longer. But I had some work I had to attend to.

Amma made *kadhi* (a curried dish made of gram flower or *besan* in a sour curd base) and rice for lunch the next day. She had also made *gajar halwa* (carrot pudding, made laboriously) that was always my favourite sweet. Baoji had a day off on Wednesday and his shift was due to change on Thursday when he had to start work at 4:00 pm. So this evening he had all the time in the world. He seemed to be in a happy mood. He had a couple of drinks and then he wanted to play the new records on the gramophone. I offered to play them, but he insisted that he would play. He first listened to Saigal's record and there was nothing stopping a flood of appreciative exclamations from him. The gramophone needed rewinding. He replaced

Saigal's record with Talat's. He liked "Shame Gham ki kasam". He had been drinking at the same time. When he flipped the record, he accidentally banged his hand into the arm of the needle. Unfortunately, the playing arm and needle came down on the record with force. The record broke in two pieces. He was totally shaken up and starting cursing himself: *"Mera beta itne pyar se mere liye record laya aur mujh bewaqoof ne use tod diya"* ("My son so lovingly brought the records for me and idiot me broke it."). It was very difficult to calm him down. He finally calmed down. I played some other records for him. Then we ate and finally went to bed.

In the morning he apologized again. I assured him that I would get that record from Delhi. During the day I spent a lot of time with Amma. She seemed worried about Baoji's throat and his difficulty in swallowing food. I assured her that he would be alright. Baoji was reading one of the novels brought by him. After lunch he had a short nap before he went for his duty. My train was at 6:30 pm. I had an early supper and then packed my luggage. Baoji sent a porter from the railway station to carry my baggage. It was so cold that Baoji was wearing his full black woolen uniform. I said goodbye to Amma, touched her feet and walked to the station. The train was on time. I touched Baoji's feet and climbed the train. Baoji gave the green flag and the train started moving.

Suddenly, Baoji pulled out the red flag and asked the caboose guard to stop the train. Baoji said he would be back in two minutes. He ran to the quarter, spent a minute there, and ran back to my compartment. I got really worried and came down on the platform. He filled my jacket's right pocket with cashews and the left pocket with *chilgoze* (pine nuts). He was out of breath but smiling. He brushed my hair with his hands, asked me to go up in the compartment. He then waved the green flag again and asked the guard to move the train. I was deeply touched with this gesture by Baoji. This was one of the most tender and unforgettable moments of my early life. I was back in Delhi next morning. The weather changed in two days with the sun coming out and the fog dissipating.

Much before my trip to Makhi, Rajeev had started looking for other job possibilities. Rajeev got an excellent job offer as a senior architect with Hindustan Steel in Ranchi. After much discussion and deliberation he decided to take the offer and moved to Ranchi alone in October of 1961. There was, of course, the issue that had to do with Saloni Bhabhi's place of residence in Delhi as she had just started her master's program in Hindi at Delhi University. Quite surprisingly, Amar happily agreed to let Saloni stay in the Roop Nagar flat. The rest of the academic year went well. However, Chachaji got very sick during the winter of 1961-62. The severe winter of Delhi was hard on his asthma. He was admitted to Patel Chest Institute. Hari, Amar and I visited him in turn and home cooked food was taken to him twice every day. It took him close to two months to fully recover.

Amar had planned a family trip to Dalhousie in Himachal Pradesh in the summer of 1962. Bhabhi, Babboo, Karuna and I went with Amar on this trip. The trip had been planned well in advance and we were to spend a month there. Bhabhi did the kitchen planning for the trip, with a burlap sack full of pots and pans, dishes and cutlery and another sack of ration supplies. We took the train from Delhi to Pathankot with a free pass courtesy of Baoji. In Pathankot we ate a sweet dish called *Palangtod* (literally meaning that one sleeps after eating this; it is a form of milk cake) and a big glass of *dahi* (yoghurt) *lassi* (shake). It was already past 2 o'clock in the afternoon when we took the bus for Dalhousie. It was a five-hour journey on a winding road, going up about 4,500 feet above Pathankot. Many people in the bus got sick, including Bhabhi and Karuna. It was a picturesque drive but not kind on the stomachs. We finally reached Dalhousie past 7 pm.

It had been a long and tiring day. In Dalhousie the streets were narrow. We had to hire a hand-pulled cart to take our baggage from the bus stop to where our accommodation had been booked. Since we were all tired, Amar decided to get the food from outside. There was one large room that we all shared. Everybody had a separate bed. There was a bathroom and running water. A part of the room was earmarked for kitchen. A makeshift curtain was created between Amar, Bhabhi and Babboo on one side and Karuna and I on the other.

In a couple of days we settled to a healthy routine. I walked a lot in Dalhousie. There were some amazingly beautiful sights, deep valleys if one walked away from the centre of the town, small ponies carrying heavy loads, an occasional white mountain horse, and nice architecture. Amar found card playing friends, some of whom he knew from Delhi. I had always enjoyed playing cards, especially rummy. Some afternoons, after lunch, Bhabhi, Karuna and I played a game called *Teen Do Panch* (Three Two Five) that is played with only 30 cards. Players take turns when they need to make two, three, and five hands. The player who calls the trump has to make five hands, and the dealer has to make only two hands. Both Bhabhi and Karuna were smart players of this game. More often than not I was the big loser. But in rummy, it was not easy to beat me.

Babboo was now five years old. I used to frequently take him for long walks. I also played ball with him, throwing and catching. He loved to play with marbles. I had already given him my entire marble collection. Once a week there was a free open air film shown free. Karuna and I never missed one. One day while on an evening walk I ran into a familiar face. This was Dr. P.C. Biswas, the head of my department at Delhi University. Neither of us expected to see each other in Dalhousie. I said "Namastey". He smiled and spoke in half English-half Bengali: "Hey Sharma, *then to bhalo*" ("Is everything okay"). He was holidaying with his family, as I was. We once again exchanged pleasantries and walked in different directions.

One day all of us went for a hiking picnic. From Dalhousie we climbed almost 2,000 feet. It was a cooler and cloudy day. It took us almost two and a half hours to go to the top of the climb, around 8,000 feet above the sea level. The place was lush green and looked like a golf course. We climbed another 300 to 400 feet when we reached a tank, called *Dahina Kund*. There was some water in the *Kund* (pond), likely from the rains. If one were to descend on the other side of the *Kund,* one could reach the district town of Chamba in less than two hours. I wanted to go there but was not allowed to go. At that height I got excited and started to run coming down. Soon I was flying like a helicopter, tumbled several times, fell down, and broke my glasses. It was an accident, so I was spared the wrath of Amar. I had a corn on the sole of my left foot. I was wearing a pair of runners. The left shoe came out, the corn opened up and there was heavy bleeding. Somehow Karuna and Bhabhi managed to cover the wound with short, clean towel. It was tough putting the shoe on. After a lot of struggle I managed to put the shoe on. Luckily I had brought with me a cane because of the corn. The cane helped a lot. But going down was slow for me. After reaching Dalhousie I had to get the dressing done at a medical facility. It took two days to get the broken lens in my glasses.

Amar did a lot of sketches and drawings with pencil on drawing paper. He had brought an easle and other art supplies with him. These sketches eventually formed the basis of about two dozen water colour paintings that he exhibited at the AIFACS gallery in New Delhi in the winter of 1962. After a month's stay in Dalhousie, we retuned to Delhi before the arrival of the monsoon rains. It was oppressively hot in Delhi with temperature hovering around 40 C and higher. The rains finally came in the third week of June. This brought much relief from the heat. During our absence, Baoji had sent a large basketful of Dashehri mangoes (one of the very best variety), about 20 kilograms in weight. Hari went to the Delhi railway station to pick up the mango basket. We returned just in time to relish them.

While teaching at Delhi School of Social Work, located outside the campus on Mall Road, Hari began to establish himself as a top class writer of Hindi short stories. He had published in many reputable magazines In 1960, he had also published a short illustrated (by Amar) book in Hindi titled *Hamare Adivasi* (Our Aboriginals), which sold many copies in schools. He was already known as a progressive individual who was way different from the norm. He was a good speaker in both Hindi and English. He had penetrating eyes and a charismatic personality. Many women liked him. He dated a few, but not to the point of full commitment. He was a member of many organizations, both national and international. One of these organizations was "Sarvas" which made it possible for individuals from a country to visit other countries. Affiliated members of the member countries served as hosts to the visitors. We had a number of such visitors, all women, come and stay in our house. One of these women was Grace Horowitz, a white Jewish woman from U.S.A. Hari became very close to her. Whether there was any commitment between them no body knew.

After a few months of stay in India, Grace returned to the U.S.A. In the autumn of 1962, Hari published one of his most powerful Hindi story titled *"Wapasi"* ("Coming Back") whose impact on the literary readership was not fully recognized until after Hari had left India for U.S.A. in 1963. He was the first in the family to leave India.

Baoji's health began to deteriorate. His throat problem was much more serious than anybody had guessed or anticipated.

14

RANGPURI AND BAOJI'S SICKNESS

I was now in the final year of my master's program in anthropology. We had to declare our specialization this year. I chose sociocultural anthropology. All those who made this choice concentrated on courses in this sub-discipline as required by the syllabus. Our main instructors that year were Dr. J. D. Mehra and Prof. R.D. Sanwal. Jaswant Yadav, Joseph Karinattu, Moorthy, Nalini Oje, Krishna Dasgupta, Subhashini Khullar, Manjit Kaur, and I took all the social anthropology classes on offer. There were other students (specializing in physical anthropology/archaeology) who took these classes as well, as indeed we all took some classes in physical anthropology/archaeology. In the first term the entire class had to undertake fieldwork for eight weeks that was to form the basis for our master's theses.

The initial plan was to go to Chakrata in the Ladakh region for the purpose of doing fieldwork. The two specialist groups had already received quite rigorous training in field methods for two months. I read, as did others, *Notes and Queries in Anthropology* published by the Royal Anthropological Institute of Great Britain and Ireland. In the classroom we learned how to collect genealogies, collect and/or use census data, how to photograph, what to photograph and what not to photograph, interviewing techniques for groups and individuals, observation, and participant observation, identification and use of key informants, and how to do all of these ethically.

But our initial plans faced an insurmountable hurdle. We had bought winter clothing and boots for the Ladakh weather. Unfortunately war broke out between China and India in early October. All civilian access to the Ladakh region was denied. It put a huge dent on our spirits. Some people talked about there being no fieldwork and students writing theses based on library research. It was just then that the ever so resourceful Dr. Mehra came up with a plan B. He had a school friend from the village Rangpuri that was located in the Union Territory of Delhi off the Mehrauli-Palam road, not far from the Delhi international airport. After some negotiation, Dr. Mehra's friend, Pandit Ram Swaroop convinced the village elders and the *Panchayat* (statutory village council) members that it would be great to host a team of students from Delhi University for a period of eight weeks. Ram Swaroop took the role of the chief host. We were all relieved and thanked our host and Dr. Mehra to salvage our fieldwork.

Rangpuri was accessible by bus but the bus dropped passengers off at a traffic crossing, called Dairee, where some shops were located, a tea stall, a cigarette and betel leaf shop, a cobbler, and a *dhaba* (road side restaurant). Rangpuri was located a little over a kilometer from Dairee. One could walk on the road towards Mehrauli and then, opposite a larger village Mahipalpur, turn right on a recently paved road to Rangpuri that ended at the southwestern edge of the village. Or, one could take a shortcut near Palam Potteries, a *pagdandi* (a pedestrian walkway), and cut across the fields and reach the village at the corner where the pond and the Boy's primary school were located.

Anthropologists, while doing fieldwork, whether they are young or old, usually stay in the location and community they are studying But this was not an option for our group of eight students that had four male and four females, unrelated to each other. There was no running water or sanitary latrines in Rangpuri households in 1962. With the exception of Jaswant Yadav and me, none of the others had ever lived in a village or relieved themselves out in the open fields. So, daily commute to the village was the only option. All of us assembled at 7:30 in the morning near Rivoli cinema in Cannaught place. Dr. Mehra's house was nearby. There were eleven of us: Dr. Mehra, Prof. Sanwal, eight of us, and a visiting female student from U.S.A., named Linda who was well over six feet tall. It is difficult to imagine how the eleven of us fitted in one car made to accommodate five people in a rather tight manner. Of course, nobody wore seat belts those days, and several individuals were sitting on others' laps, thighs or knees. It was indeed very tight and uncomfortable. But it was a short 25-minute ride from Cannaught Place. We somehow managed.

One evening just before returning to the city, we found that we had a flat tire. There was no service station within a few kilometers, so we had to use a bicycle hand pump to put some air in the leaking tire, enough to take us to the nearest service station. Dr. Mehra did not have a spare tire in the trunk. We had to refill the air three times into the leaking tire before we managed to reach the service station. But we just laughed it off as one of "those" unexpected incidents. Linda was the first and only casualty of the fieldwork experience. Being a tall person she was very uncomfortable in the car. As a smoker, she was made fun of since smoking by a woman was such an oddity and rare thing at the time. She used to wear skirts without pantyhose. Curious village boys will follow her. Some will yell: *"Are mem aa gayi"* ("Hey, the white woman has arrived"). Some dare devil boys would even walk to her and run their hands on her bare legs. After five days of visiting Rangpuri, Linda decided against coming there any more.

All students chose different research problems for their fieldwork. For example, Yadav was examining the village and its extensions to the outside world. Joseph was looking at the role of religion in village life. I decided to focus on family, marriage, and kinship among the largest caste group in Rangpuri, the Jats. Rangpuri was a village of medium size and had a population of 1,986 people in 1962. It had eight *jati* (or sub-caste) groupings consisting of Brahman, *Jat* (landowner/farmer), *Nai* (barber), *Sakka* (water carrier), *Manihar* (bangle supplier), *Kumhar* (potter), *Chamar* (leather worker), and *Bhangi* (sweeper/scavenger). There was also a *Khati* (carpenter) who rented accommodation in a Jat household, but he was not a permanent resident. For services of occupational specialist caste groups that were not present in Rangpuri, the village residents had to rely on members of these groups in other villages. The *jajmani* system of inter-caste dependence existed whereby landless lower castes, known as *kamins*, provided goods and/or services to landowning upper castes, known as *jajmans*, and in return were paid, not in cash, but in kind, that is a traditionally and historically agreed upon portion of the harvested crop.

Our fieldwork was going well. We had so much to do in so little time. Our professors, Mehra and Sanwal, were so very helpful, providing guidance, support, pointers, and advice. They kept us anchored and clearly focused. They also made tea for the students. We all brought our lunch from our homes, pooled the food and shared at lunchtime. Sometimes we stayed in Rangpuri until almost 8 pm. By the time we reached out respective homes, it was pretty late, often approaching 10 pm or later. Sunday was the only day we did not go to Rangpuri, although Yadav and I made it to the village even on some Sundays. We will take a bus up to Dairee and then walk to the village. By the end of the second week, I was pretty much entrapped in the grueling fieldwork routine. Collecting genealogies is a time-consuming and cumbersome task. I searched and found four key informants and spent long hours with each one of them. I also did house to house census of the village, drew a map, and took photographs of people, cattle, agricultural tools and public buildings.

The situation at home had become very tense. Baoji's discomfort in swallowing food had exacerbated. The railway doctors believed that something sinister was going on in Baoji's throat region, but they could not pin it down. He was put on medical leave. He came to Delhi. Amar and Hari took him to Ganga Ram Hospital where Baoji had a biopsy done. The biopsy revealed that he had a cancerous growth at the root of the tongue that had been causing him pain and discomfort. The cancer was at a fairly advanced stage. As a long shot Baoji underwent a surgical procedure at Safdarjung Hospital. But this too did not help. Baoji returned to Makhi. He then spent three weeks in Lucknow Medical College undergoing extensive radiation treatment. He made a quick trip to Bawal and then returned to Makhi and resumed his duties once again.

Baoji used to write me letters at my department of anthropology address. Here is one of his letters:

"Om"

Makhi

D/10.11.62

My dear son Satya Prakash

God may keep you healthy, happy, cheerful, hail, hearty and prosperous. I have received your one card and one long letter which have pleased me much. I have also sent a letter on or about 28th or 29th at the address of Roop Nagar addressed to all of you. Find out if it is not misdelivered. I have been in lot of pain quite intolerable since I returned back from Delhi but quite fortunately and all of a sudden I am feeling quite better today and only today. Now let us see if this sudden change remains or again turns to adverse. I have also received letters of Hari Prakash and [Amar] and on receipt of [Amar's] letter I wrote that letter on 28th or 29th. If this condition which is today proves to be permanent then great many thanks to God. I intend to go to Lucknow to see the therapist next month after expiry of complete three months from the treatment for checkup.

I have noted your sentiments and love and regard for me with great satisfaction and compliance. I have given up drinking from 13/8/62 the day treatment started nd continued it right up to the day when I purchased a half bottle of Solan whiskey from Rewari on getting my pension on 9/10/62 for which an idea had been developed in my mind to see what reaction it gives to me. It was only a matter of chance. So I used it for two days on 9th and 10th which gave me neither good nor bad reaction and since then I have not touched it and now intend to leave it all for the whole of my life. Although I keep smoking few *biris* which I cannot help and that does not give me any irritation and excitement apparently. Let God give me the strength to keep to this to the mark and point.

I do not agree with you that my sons are quite obedient and respectful. When a son can say that we should not dare to see the door of his house what else is required. We are tired of hearing such derogatory, insulting and humiliating words and behaviour and no more capacity for the same. One son passes just close by three times and does not care to visit his ailing father with severe and dangerous trouble and disease what can be expected from them. They do not hesitate to behave in any way they like and have been bad naming us here and there to all concerned. So it is their viewpoint and are at liberty because they are now grown up and have attained good honourable position and status.

After all I wish that they should and may keep healthy, happy, cheerful and with ever rising prosperity and good luck. This is the only source of our pleasure.

Please send my old warm suit of daily use by parcel immediately as it was left by your mother as she was quite upset by the words of [Amar] that day. This suit is needed by me urgently. Eating and speaking are still giving me trouble as the tongue is still not working properly

Your program of going to Chakrata has also been cancelled and now you will do fieldwork in the village near Delhi. This has pleased me very much.. Take all care of your health and studies and write me if you require any thing (including money) without hesitation.

Reply welfare.

Very affectionately yours,

K.L. Sharma

This letter from Baoji broke my heart. I cried a lot. But I did not share this letter with anyone. The letter was a testimony to Baoji's badly hurt feelings, that too at a time when he was facing the biggest battle of his life. I couldn't even think of who to blame for his predicament. I felt so helpless.

Amma, and, to a lesser extent, Baoji were in denial about the final outcome. He went to Lucknow for a check-up and was told that there was nothing further they could do for him. He was advised to go to Delhi. Hari went to Makhi and brought him to Delhi. The household things were moved to Bawal. Amma also came to Delhi. Baoji was in a lot of pain and his ability to swallow food was diminishing, slowly but steadily. To cope with the pain, the doctors had started giving him morpheme. I spent as much time with Baoji as I could. He seemed very interested in my fieldwork and asked many, many questions. I would describe for him everything I did on a given day. He would sometimes say he was very proud of me.

Baoji slept in the middle bedroom. There were two beds in the room, one always there and was meant for Baoji. The other one was a cot that was brought into the room at bedtime and Amma used that for sleeping. During daytime there were usually two chairs near Baoji's bed. During my fieldwork in Rangpuri, Baoji spent all day and night in the middle room. He was able to walk to the toilet for natural calls. Occasionally, and especially on Sundays, he will either sit on a chair in the sun or lie on a cot in the courtyard. Baoji always asked me to cut his nails and massage his head with mustard oil. I was an expert in cutting his finger nails, even toe nails, using just a bare razor blade. I did not have access to a nail cutter. Despite swallowing difficulties, he was able to eat soft food until mid-December of 1962. Amar was now very mallow in his interaction with Baoji. His relationship with Rajeev had also considerably improved. He even escorted Saloni to Ranchi for Christmas holidays in 1961. This was indeed a sea change. There is much truth in the wise saying that calamity and crises can bring members of the family closer.

Back in Rangpuri, Yadav and I often had to help Joseph Karinattu with his interviewing. Joseph could barely speak a few words and sentences in Hindi. Religion is a difficult topic to research on, especially when one is examining the relationship between the Great and Little traditions of Hinduism, the former dealing with the textual interpretation and the latter with the contextual reality. Everyone on the team helped out Joseph, playing the role of interpreter for him. One day, Yadav got into a tight spot with an elderly Jat man who was a retired *subedar* from the Indian army. Both were hot tempered. Yadav was asking *subedar* Dilip Singh questions about his landholding. As the war with China was still going on, the *subedar* suspected Yadav to be a Chinese spy and, having lost his cool, he pulled out his service revolver. By coincidence, and luckily, Pt. Ram Swaroop and I were walking, right at that moment, in front of Dilip Singh's *baithak*, (men's area in front of the house) as I was being escorted to the house of a completely new (to me) informant. The high commotion made us stop and we were immensely helpful in calming both Yadav and the *subedar*. In no time they were shaking each other's hands. Sometimes a slight misunderstanding can create an ugly incidence in fieldwork.

One morning in Rangpuri I was told by one of my informants that there were two young Jat women from Bawal, my own native town, actual sisters in fact, one of whom was blind, were married to one Jat man in Rangpuri. This surprised me because while it was quite common among the Jats for two (even more than two in some cases) sisters to be married at the same time to two (or more) Jat men who were actual brothers, it was unheard of that one man would have two sisters as his multiple wives which was the case with the sisters from Bawal. The practice of two or more brothers marrying two or more sisters at the same time, it was explained to me, existed because it was economical—one *baraat,* one priest, shared dowry, etc.—and also because the sisters will keep their in-laws's family united. But in this case, it was one man who had married both sisters. Legally, Hindus can have only one wife at a time, although serial monogamy is permitted. The older sister was blind from birth and no one wanted to marry her. The step taken by the Jat man from Rangpuri was both charitable and progressive.

When I shared this information with Prof. Sanwal, he advised me to go visit my "sisters" because all females born within your village, were, through fictive kinship, your sisters, and further to give them some token gift (as from brother to sister). Next day, I visited the house of those sisters and told them that I was from Bawal and gave them five rupees each. The news of this gift spread like a prairie fire and, thanks to Prof. Sanwal, greatly helped enhance my rapport with residents of Rangpuri. I became known as someone who knew village customs quite well. This was not something that a book taught you. I came to the realization that each fieldwork situation dictates its own terms and that no one fieldwork experience is like another one. At any rate, there were no fieldwork manuals available in 1962. There were also few, if any, published works that dealt with moral and ethical principles of doing fieldwork.

As the fieldwork was winding up, I did my best to spend time with Baoji. Almost every day he was getting increasingly fragile and losing weight. Once a week I will give him a shave. As it was getting colder towards the end of November, Baoji wanted to lie down in the sun. Amma, I, or someone else in the family would make a bed for him on a cot in the courtyard. Baoji would occasionally read the newspaper or a novel from the library. His energy was beginning to sap and he tired easily and quickly. Occasionally he would dose off with his reading glasses on. After a short nap, he would call me and ask how my research was proceeding. He knew I had to soon start analyzing my research data and start writing my M.A. thesis. He would almost daily insist not to worry about him and spend as much time at the university library as possible so that my studies and thesis would not be neglected. Almost as my personal responsibility I made sure that Saloni Bhabhi stayed in the library and studied as I did. There was no place any more in the house to study for either of us.

When Manju learned about Baoji's sickness, she came to visit and sat beside Baoji. She did that a few times. During one visit, she had her brother, Rajat, and her mother accompany her. From Baoji's eyes I could read that he liked Manju. There was not much celebration for my birthday on January 1, 1963. Amma made *kheer* (rice pudding). But Baoji could barely taste it. Whatever he tried to eat or drink, more than two-thirds came out. One could read the pain and agony on his face. Our hearts cried out for him. In order to work on my thesis, attend classes, and keep up with studies generally kept me away from home a substantial part of most days. I also had to make up two trips to Rangpuri to fill up some blanks in my fieldwork data. My mentor in writing my thesis was Prof. Sanwal who lived in Model Town. I made several visits, using my bicycle, to his house on Sundays to seek advice and clarification on some kinship concepts and relating them to my fieldwork. The thesis, typed and bound, had to be submitted by the end of February. So, it was hard work all the way.

One day, a bright and sunny afternoon in January, Baoji lying on the bed in the courtyard signaled me to come close to him. He could not say very much because of his condition. First he asked me to cut his nails that I did. Then he looked straight into my eyes with a "thank you" type gratitude. Then he gestured to me to bring his reading glasses, writing pad, and pen. I supported him with pillows in a half lying position. He scribbled a couple of sentences on the paper. "I want to live. Please get me operated upon. This pain is intolerable." I started crying. None of the brothers were at home. I went out to see Dr. Khanna who wrote prescriptions for Baoji. I showed him Baoji's note. He said there was not much that could be done for Baoji and that he would die soon, may be in a couple of weeks or so. He came home to inject Baoji with a morpheme shot. He told me to give him whatever he wanted, an alcoholic drink, a cigarette, or more morpheme injections. According to Dr. Khanna, Baoji was reaching the end. When he left, I went into the corner room, shut the doors and cried a lot. Crying was all one could do.

It was a very stress-filled time for the whole family. Laughter had disappeared. Even conversations were brief, in low, almost hushed, tones.

Amma was no longer in denial. We all knew the eventual outcome. We all know when we are born, but death takes its own course: cruel, yet undeniable. Everyone has to die, but when and how cannot be predicted or forecasted with any degree of certainty. Life starts the cycle; death ends it. Those who die are gone forever. But they leave behind memories, good and bad, happy and sad. Often these memories sustain the survivors. But no two survivors are alike. But sooner or later, life does go on. That is the fact of life. But I did not understand all this in 1963. The only thing I knew was that I loved my father immensely and watching him waste away physically was one of the most difficult experiences of my life.

Being busy, first with fieldwork, then analyzing data and writing the thesis, while at the same time worrying about Baoji's fast deteriorating health left very little if any, "me" time. I had not seen a movie in close to three months, something of a record for me. Saloni had asked me if it would be okay to go see a movie. I responded by saying that I could not get around to doing that under the circumstances. I had a deadline to meet. There was no thesis requirement for doing a Master's degree in Hindi. I also could not afford to miss a class as this was the busy final year. I was also, whenever time would allow, preparing myself for the final examination. My method in studying for the final examination involved formulating a set of questions for each paper, doing all the necessary research, and then writing the essays in response to those questions.

An eerie silence in the family had just about become the norm. Food did not taste that good any more, especially for me when I looked at

Baoji who could not pass anything down his throat. Bhabhi, Amar's wife, was expecting her second child, due in May. Amma began to make extra effort to help with the household chores, aside from taking care of Baoji around the clock. The end could come any time now. Amar and Hari would leave instructions for Bhabhi every morning. She was to call them right away if the situation got worse. Hari was still working with the Delhi School of Social Work, whereas Amar still taught at Ludlow Castle near Kashmiri Gate. We did not have a phone in the house. Hari still frequently used the bicycle or the bus. Amar rode his scooter to work. As for myself, I usually walked to the Delhi University campus along with Saloni. Karuna took the bus to Delhi Polytechnic located near Kashmiri Gate. She was almost everyday accompanied by her college mate, Manju. She came to our flat every morning from the back door to walk with Karuna to the bus stop. Catching a glimpse of Manju's beautiful face used to be the only major highlight of the day for me. I had begun to like her.

15

HE IS NO MORE

I got really busy in my thesis work as preparation of genealogical diagrams and kinship terminological charts consumed a good deal of time. On the morning of February12, 1963, Baoji summoned me through gesturing and asked for his glasses, paper and pen. With very unsteady hands, he first wrote: "Please get surgery done; I want to live." He took off his glasses and was about to lie down, but stopped, Putting glasses back again, he scribbled: "Send a telegram to Rajeev and ask him to come immediately. I want to see him." He collapsed with exhaustion, lied down and closed his eyes. I immediately bicycled to the telegram office near Palace cinema and sent the telegram. I did not tell anyone else that I had done so.

February 14 was a nice sunny day. For me it started out ominously. Not many people knew about Valentine's Day in India those days. By and large, Delhi University was a very conservative campus those days. Male and female students never went past holding hands. Only males smoked; smoking by females was very rare. Young women wore saris, and salwar-kameez, and skirts were as rare as hails on a sunny day. Romancing was not uncommon, but public gestures of intimacy were rare. For young men and women, film actors provided the role models, as indeed they do now. The only drinks one could have on and off campus were tea, coffee, cold drinks, and shakes. The middle class did not have much disposable income. Luxury goods were hard to get, both in terms of accessibility and affordability. Moving to "wants" was a rare occurrence; only the very rich could afford it.

I was shaving just before 8 am. I suddenly heard the front gate of the flat open and I saw Kaushalya Bhua walk in. This was quite odd, because Bhua never came unexpectedly. I had a hunch that something terrible was going to happen during the day. I walked toward the kitchen where Amar and Hari were having breakfast. I expressed my unwillingness to go to the university that day. But they both exhorted me to go to the campus and not to worry about anything. Manju was already there, waiting for Karuna to walk to the bus stop. I quickly had a bath, got dressed and walked to the campus with Saloni. I wasn't keen to go that day. Rajeev had not yet arrived from Ranchi either.

Upon reaching the campus, I went to the Department of Anthropology library and studied for a while. It was already time for Prof. Sanwal's class in social anthropology. The lecture dealt with culture change among the *adivasis* (aboriginals) of India. I sat next to Jaswant Yadava. My concentration was lacking but I still took down the notes, using my fountain pen. Ballpoints were unheard of those days. Exactly at 10:24 am the fountain pen slipped out of my hand and fell to the ground. I was shaken up. The nib of the fountain pen had broken. Prof. Sanwal looked at me and asked: "Are you okay Sharma?" My response was in the affirmative. Prof. Sanwal offered me his pen that I accepted with thanks. At the end of the class I returned the pen and walked to another room with Yadava for the next class, this one on physical anthropology by Dr. Indera Pal Singh Monga. My attention was still distracted but I was writing notes from the lecture. About midway through the class, Yadava drew my attention to the classroom's door. Hari was standing there, wearing *kurta* and *paijama*, with red eyes and unruly hair. He swung his head sideways, indicating that Baoji had passed away. My heart started beating faster. I collected my things and excused myself from the class. Hari hugged me hard in the corridor and told me that Baoji had passed away at 10:24 am. He asked me to get Saloni from her class and go home as soon as possible. I was wearing pants and jacket. Hari instructed me to change into white *kurta* and *paijama* as soon as I got home. I broke the news to Saloni and she started crying too. From Maurice Nagar we fetched an auto and got home in about five minutes.

The home scene was quite chaotic. I immediately changed and came to the front courtyard where Baoji's body had already been taken off the bed and put on the ground. His fragile body, with eyes closed, was covered by a white bedsheet. There were already a number of people in the house, including Ram Kumar Chachaji and Chachi. Rajeev had still not arrived. Amar instructed me to take the bicycle and go to Delhi Polytechnic at Kashmiri Gate to bring Karuna home. I biked as hard as I could the more than five kilometer distance. I parked the bike and went to Karuna's classroom. A lecture was in session. I knocked at the door. The instructor asked who I was. I told him that I was Karuna's brother and had come to fetch Karuna and take her home as our father had passed away. The class was shocked by my saying this loudly for all to hear. Karuna started crying loudly. I hugged her. She put all her things in the shoulder bag and came with me. I asked her to sit on the bar connected to the handles of the bicycle, and raced back on the bike to get to home.

This time, upon reaching home, I cried very hard. I thought I had lost the most precious thing in my life. It felt that life was not worth living without Baoji. As the oldest son, Amar was to carry out the role of the chief mourner. A barber was called home. Amar's head and moustache were shaved by a knife. He then took a bath and wore white Kurta and paijama. It was his job now to bathe Baoji's body and to dress him up in new clothes. Hari and I had to help Amar in dressing Baoji's body. Then a stretcher was made to carry him on the shoulders. Rajeev was still not there. We decided to wait for him for another two hours when the next train was expected to reach Delhi railway station. But he did not come. Apparently the telegram somehow reached him late or something like that had happened. It was getting late and we could not wait any more as the body had to be cremated before sundown.

My friend Yadava had come too. Among the people who had assembled at home I also saw Manju along with her mother. There were close to 40 people who had gathered to take the dead body of Baoji to *shamshaan ghaat* (cremation ground) at the banks of the Yamuna River. Women did not go to the cremation ground. That was the traditional cultural norm. Just before four o'clock we started our trek to the cremation ground, four shoulders carrying Baoji's body and frequently changing shoulders as a long distance had to be covered. Throughout the trek we kept reciting *"Ram naam satya hai."* ("God's name is the truth."). Amar lit the fire to the wood covering the body. It didn't take very long for the body to burn out. The presiding priest who did *pooja* and recited *mantras* was given *dakshina* (service fee), and fruits were fed to the large number of monkeys present at the *ghaat*. Afterwards, we walked home.

A life, a precious life, had ended. We all now had to pick up the pieces and start life without our father. Rajeev arrived by the late night train. Everybody felt sad that he could not see Baoji before he had passed away. But destiny somehow dictates what comes to happen. It took a lot of time to recover mentally. I still had to complete a thesis, defend it and write the examination papers. To make matters worse, soon after I completed my thesis and submitted bound copies to the department, I came down with chicken pox. I had to contend with uncomfortable chicken pox boils that were itchy and high fever. Karuna also got chicken pox a few days later. We had two cots side by side in the middle room. I could not shave for close to a month. A comforting grace was the sight of Manju who often came to visit Karuna, and occasionally spoke to me about my health. Somehow, I was even more attracted to her.

While I always believed that people are architects of their own fate, deep inside me I began to concede that destiny plays an important role too. The sadness came from Baoji's death as I could no longer share anything with him.

EPILOGUE

As I write this, Baoji left us 53 years ago. Ram Kumar Chachaji also died the same year as Baoji, in 1963. I still miss Baoji a lot and light a candle in front of his photograph on every anniversary of his death. A lot has happened since his death. Hari was the first to leave India for U.S.A. for further studies and a great teaching career as a professor of sociology and a political activist in Vancouver, Canada. Amar was the next to leave India on a Fulbright scholarship to an American university. Later in his life he became a very successful artist. Rajeev was the next to leave, first for London, and then to U.S.A. He made a flourishing career as a highly successful architect in a small town in upstate New York. I was the last to leave India, also as a Fulbright scholar, and attended Cornell University for graduate work in anthropology. Later I moved to Canada in 1970 and have lived there since then. Karuna married an air force officer and made a successful career herself as an artist and a teacher.

And, yes, I did marry Manju and had a wonderful married life with two kids. Amma, my great mother and a strong lady, survived for a long time after Baoji's death. She lived life on her own terms. So much she taught us. I was lucky to bring her to Canada in 1977 where she spent three years, circulating periodically between Rajeev, Hari and me. But she was an Indian at core, returned there in 1980 and lived alone in Bawal until her death in 1992.

The biggest regret is that Baoji could not see us flourish in the manner we did. He would have been so proud of us all, and proud also because he brought us into this world. A number of people have left the Sharma clan. Manju passed away in 2009. Hari left us in 2010 and so did Binno just three months later. Amar's wife, Sanyukta, who was a second mother to me, passed away last year. Old people pass on and new ones are born. Such is the rhythm of nature. But memories do not die for the living. Many in my present extended family never met Baoji. This novel will make them aware of him and give them a sense of their roots and heritage. My Baoji was not an easy person to decipher. But deep down he was a very compassionate individual who, despite his lack of financial security, enjoyed life to the fullest. That is his greatest legacy. I wish I could have a drink with him.

Surrey, B.C., Canada

March 15, 2016

The End

Printed in the United States
By Bookmasters